THE THRESHING:

A Weapon Forged By Fire

A Survivor's Story

Marsha and Samuel Winters

Exulon
ELITE

THE THRESHING:
A Weapon Forged By Fire
by Marsha and Samuel Winters

Printed in the United States of America

ISBN 9781498404266

www.xulonpress.com

I give this book to God to do with it as He wills. I have placed my most painful, embarrassing moments of life on paper for all to see. I pray to be used as a tool to set others free from the same chains that once held me down. I dedicate this to all those who have been broken, battered and bruised by life's struggles and the grip of sin. Your rejection, insecurities and fear are the perfect ingredients needed to make you into a warrior for the Lord. You are a weapon in the making; you just need to realize it.

FOREWORD

*W*hen I first met Marsha Winters eight years ago I thought to myself, "Here is a woman – strong, regal, and proud – someone with whom you do not want to mess." There was not even a hint of the "victim" in her bearing or presentation – nothing to indicate she had ever been traumatized by the unspeakable actions of others. It wasn't because she was putting on airs or playacting for my benefit or in an attempt to convince me I should hire her husband as our church's new youth pastor – it was simply because she was "pressing on" to take hold of that for which Christ Jesus took hold of her (Philippians 3:12). Instead of clinging to the past and allowing it to define her present and her future, she had already decided to move forward – and more importantly – to move toward Christ, knowing that every step she took in His direction was one more step away from all the enemy had intended for evil in her life.

Of course, that was eight years ago. Since then, she and I have messed with each other quite a bit! She's plastered my car with bumper stickers and trained her two youngest children – from the time they were infants – to call me "Monkey." In turn, when she was waiting for the results of her immigration exam, I had someone call her impersonating an immigration officer to let her know she had failed the test (she didn't really). There's more, but in Marsha's words, they're not my stories to tell.

Strong, regal, proud – but also fun, loving, loyal and powerfully spiritual – that's Marsha. God's not finished with her just yet. She's still not all she's going to be, but her life story is an indisputable testament to the truth of these song lyrics –

All I had to offer Him was brokenness and strife But He made something beautiful of my life.[1]

Rev. Dominick A. Scibetta – Pastor

Assembly of God

---

1 Lyrics by Gloria Gaither / Music by Bill Gaither / Copyright © 1971

CONTENTS

INTRODUCTION

MY INSPIRATION

"Behold, I will make thee a new sharp threshing instrument having teeth: thou shalt thresh the mountains, and beat them small, and shalt make the hills as chaff." Isaiah 41:15 (KJV)

Thresh: To beat the stalks of ripped grain with a flail or machine so as to separate the grain from the straw or husk. The act of "threshing" is to move or thrash about.[2]

As one of my favorite Bible verses, Isaiah 41:15 has meant so much to me. It was a beacon of hope in my dimly lit world. Through my adult years when my spirit was scarred and wounded, this was the verse God gave me for comfort. I do wonder, "Why this one?"–out of all the verses to pick from. Why wouldn't God chose...

---

2 Funk and Wagnall's Standard Dictionary, 1984

"And we know that in all things God works for the good of those who love him, who have been called according to his purpose." Romans 8:28 (NIV)

Or, He could have also chosen . . .

*"They will receive blessing from the L*ORD *and vindication from God their Savior. Such is the generation of those who seek him, who seek your face, God of Jacob." Psalms 24:5-6 (NIV)*

I believe God chose to use Isaiah 41:15 because it was the key to motivate me into eventually becoming a weapon for the Kingdom. When I came to know God, I was not an instrument. I was a victim, marred and destroyed. He took something the world found unusable and changed me into a warrior.

LET'S BE CLEAR

There are two things I want you to know before we begin. First, my deepest desire is not to glorify sin or demonize any of the characters in this book. The situations and people of my past may not be glamorous, but God has used them to make me into the woman I am today. I purposely left out some details I believe are too gruesome and distasteful. It is not my desire to feed you any unnecessary gore or imagery, but only to show that God is in the business of healing, restoring and breaking the chains Satan continues to use to bind and hold people down.

Yes, there are many books out there written by those who have been through situations far greater than I. Book shelves are full of authors who have overcome the unthinkable. Some of those very books and testimonies are the tools God used to help pull me out of the pit I was in. Those very books gave me the confidence to face my past, muster up the courage, and use my experiences to help others. I have no desire or intention to out-do someone else's story, and I am not trying to embellish my own testimony to gain sympathy or popularity. I write my story purely to become a "Threshing Instrument"—not allowing the devil to take a hold over my life, but beating HIM down by helping and inspiring the people of God. If my story can help others facing situations similar to mine, or allow someone to find strength in the power of God's arms, then my job is done.

Second, in order to best tell my story, I have to mention others by name. The names of all characters in this book have been changed out of respect for them. I have even changed my own name to protect others. As I said above, it is not my wish to demonize anyone. With all that you are about to read, I have forgiven and moved on. The Lord has done a new work in me which allows me to tell these stories. A few years ago I was not strong enough to speak about these things or even recall them. Now, by writing "fake" names, I hope to protect every individual from judgment and embarrassment.

I am writing this book to several people–leaders, mature Christians, women–but to a few in particular. I am writing to help parents become alert to what their children may face each and every day. I feel that well-meaning parents have put down their guards in protecting their children's innocence. They are not aware of the challenges their children face. My story takes place several years ago and now the struggles are even greater than they were back when I was a child. This is also the time for parents to ask questions and not be afraid of knowing when something might be wrong.

I also want young people to know there is a God who hears you when you cry–who can be your cloud of peace in this world of chaos. I want you to know MY JESUS–this Jesus who held me when I was in the dirt of sin. He held me when no one else would. He loved me the way I should have been loved and He will do the same for you.

I am also talking to the person who is just tired of living like a victim, tired of being a slave to circumstances–the one who wants some control and some sense of normalcy. I want you to know that God never intended his children to be punching bags, but instead powerful warriors who tear down the gates of hell. Satan is the one who should be protecting the little he has, because we as Christians are waging war against him–but he has us convinced that he is stronger than we are. That is just not true and I pray you will find courage and confidence by the end of my story.

Part One

?

Chapter 1

I CAN'T CHANGE THE PAST

One of the worst weapons Satan can and will use against people are their own memories and thoughts. I remember a well known evangelist explaining it as a TV channel you can never change, or a movie theater from which you can never exit. He keeps playing the same scene over and over again, breaking you down every single time.

MY CHANNEL

My earliest memories begin in my home country of Jamaica, located in the West Indies. I was three years old when my parents decided it would be best for the family to leave Jamaica and move to America. The hope was that in America we would have greater opportunities and a better way of life. We already had some extended family members who made the move and they were waiting for our arrival. Unfortunately, due to certain immigration laws, my entire family could not go. My mother and I would have to go ahead while my father and older brother had to stay behind. Then, after all the paper work was cleared up, they would follow along and join us. This was the plan, but now looking back with better understanding in serving the Lord, I realize how important it is to go to God in prayer about **everything** before making life changing decisions. Unfortunately, my home was not a Christian home and God was certainly not at the center of it.

At such a young age my attachment to my brother was much stronger than the one I had with my father. My older brother was the best older brother a girl could ever have. James was seven when my mother and I left Jamaica. To this day, when I think of him at that age it brings a huge smile to my face. We were partners in crime. And he always knew how to make me laugh. (Yes, I can remember all that happened when I was just three). A life without him just did not register in my mind. I could not understand being without him. I didn't even think about leaving my father as much as I thought about leaving James.

April 15, 1981 was the day my mother had to tell James that we would not be home when he came back from school. I can't imagine what my brother was feeling. In his recollection of that day, he thought it was because of his behavior and he promised he would be a better little boy. He could not understand why she was leaving. My mother was everything to him, as every mother is meant to be to their child. He said he spent that day hoping that when he came home, she and I would be there but that was not the case. The pain he went through because of us leaving was overwhelming. I would say more, but the events that follow for James are not mine to tell.

To this day, I still do not know what gave my parents the courage to come up with the idea of not just moving to a foreign country, but also doing so without any money or resources. My mom realized immediately that this was not what she had expected. There were more challenges to face here and the opportunities were not as glamorous as the 1980's TV programs had made them seem. There were no white picket fences and there wasn't money at every corner. In Jamaica she was a teacher and she was given high respect. My mom told me one time that life in Jamaica was segregated, but not by color. You were separated by the level of education you received. As an educator, she was given a higher status than some. However, she still struggled. My father didn't finish school and had to drop out. He was able to read, but his spelling was not up to par. Life in America was hard, even harder for a noncitizen, but my mother never thought about quitting. My aunt, who took us in, helped us as much as she could. She had also left her family behind in Jamaica. For a while it was just my aunt, her daughter (who was in her early twenties), and my mother and I in a small apartment. We eventually needed to get a place of our own and my mother needed to find a job because my aunt could not carry us all on her own. My mother could not find a job as a teacher. The only jobs that became available to her were cleaning bathrooms and houses. It was all she was able to do to help provide food and save up to bring my father and brother over.

Soon after, my aunt was able to get a new apartment and sent for the rest of her family—her husband and two boys. Aaron, the oldest, was in his late teens. And Matthew, the younger, was in his early teens. My older, female cousin was able to find a roommate and moved into her own apartment. With a much fuller home to live in now, out of pure desperation, my mother decided to move into a room that was for rent. She left me with my aunt, uncle and their two boys.

Before I go on, I want to say that I would not be where I am today without the sacrifice of my aunt and uncle. They loved me and treated me as their own. My aunt was, and is, a very strong woman. She was a great example to me. My uncle was a funny and wonderful man. They tried to give me all they could while I was with them. I was even disciplined like one of their own. I remember being threatened by my aunt who said she was going to wash my mouth out with soap because I was so fresh—and I do remember eating some soap when I was with her. I know that woman loved me and she never showed anything less.

Yet, I was still left in a place of confusion that overtook me when my mother first left. I was mortified because not only was she leaving me, but she was leaving me with people I was not familiar with. And she gave no real explanation. As great as my aunt and uncle were, I still wanted my brother, I wanted my James. I wanted to go home, but instead I felt that for some reason my mom was choosing to break my heart. I was still three years old and I had no understanding of my life. My mom tried really hard to visit often. She would have dinner with us, read me stories for bedtime, and even picked me up from school at times. But why was she leaving? What was she doing that I could not go with her? I remember one day she came over for one of her visits. As the time came for her to leave, I broke down in tears. I thought that maybe if I behaved better she would not leave me and she would bring me with her. I felt absolutely helpless. There was nothing I could do to make her to stay. It didn't matter how many times she left, I never got used to it. This wasn't the normal kind of separation anxiety babies go through during a certain stage of their life, this was a total feeling of being abandoned. It hurt more and more. It didn't matter how many times my aunt and cousins tried to explain it to me. Please understand that I don't want to paint a picture of my mother that makes it seem as if she was heartless and unfeeling. Every move she made in 1981 was extremely painful for her. I know she did a lot of crying when she had to leave me, which made this all even more confusing for me.

INNOCENCE STOLEN

In time, I started to love my cousin Aaron. I was a tiny thing and it felt like everyone in the world was bigger than me. I had fun with it at times, but the biggest person to me was my Aaron. In my mind he was a strong, tall figure and he made me feel safe. Not even my aunt and uncle made me feel as safe as Aaron did. On many occasions, because I was so small, he would put me on his shoulders and carry me to wherever we were going. To this day, my family recalls how I loved him – and they were right. In a time of pure uncertainty and fear, he made me feel like all was right just by his presence. He was so patient and loving to me, and He was always so much fun. At times I would even get on his nerves, but he still made me feel good. He was the total opposite of his younger brother, Matthew, who was 13 years old. Matthew never spoke to me and wanted almost nothing to do with me. I tried to get him to like me or even talk to me, but I could tell my snappy attitude and spicy responses made him want to leave me on a corner for someone to kidnap.

I was so excited on the day he did take an interest in me. I don't remember anyone being home when he brought me in his room and asked me if I wanted to play with a new toy that had just come out, the Rubik's Cube. I couldn't believe he was letting me touch it after treating me like I had leprosy. As I was playing, he took it out of my hand and told me if I wanted to play some more I needed to do something to him. He introduced me to performing sexual acts that left nothing but more confusion in my mind. Matthew told me to keep this between us. He said that it was our secret game, and I could only have the Rubik's Cube if I continued to play these games with him. Needing acceptance from him, I did just that. I kept it between us. But afterwards there was always this feeling that would come over me. I didn't understand it. These games always left me feeling dirty. By this time I was four years old, about to turn five, and I had some feeling that what I was doing was not right, but I wanted acceptance from the one person who rejected me the most.

Let's stop here. Isn't that like Satan? Look at what he did with Adam and Eve. Genesis 3 recalls how he didn't tempt them with something they already had, but he tempted them instead with the one thing they could not have. He made these things appealing to their eyes and blinded them from the truth in front of them. He does the same with us. He draws you in and then – BOOM! – He's got you. Scripture says that after they ate of the fruit, their eyes were opened (3:7). Unlike Adam and Eve, I did not understand my actions. My intentions were purely innocent. Instead, I look at how the enemy sets his traps. He has been doing this from the beginning of time, making us think that what we don't have is worth sacrificing everything else for. Look at it. I was in a loving home with my aunt, uncle, and older cousin, but I wanted so badly for Matthew to receive me as well and just to talk to me. When tempted with something that I did not have – his acceptance – I was willing to do whatever I needed to do – and it was a detestable thing.

I would love to tell you that this one incident was the last time it happened. But Matthew did this over and over again during a 5 month time span, and increased his demands each time. He became bolder. He saw I was keeping the secret and that allowed him to gain more confidence. He would no longer wait to be alone with me in the house, he would do it with family members in the other room or kitchen. I started feeling like I couldn't do it anymore. I just didn't want to – I couldn't take it. Eventually, there was nothing with which he could bribe me to get me to do it, so he started to threaten me. I remember very clearly the day I told him "no". He responded by saying, "If you don't do it, then I will tell your mother that you weren't behaving. And you know what will happen if I tell her, she won't come to visit you." I was stunned and didn't know what to think. I thought that what he said was true. My mother was everything to me, the idea of not being able to see her was more traumatic to me than what he was making me do – so I gave in.

It wasn't long after Matthew began molesting me that I started going to the doctor. My mother could not understand it and there were things happening to me that even the doctor couldn't explain. They thought the pain I was feeling in my personal areas would get better if I just changed to different types of underwear. No one understood what was going on with me emotionally either. I started changing and I started to explore things I shouldn't have been exploring. I was getting into trouble at school for inappropriate statements. My mind became distorted and corrupt, but no one was picking up on the signs. Unfortunately, this was just the beginning.

Chapter 2

A LIFE WITHOUT UNDERSTANDING

DAD COMES HOME

Life continued on even though I felt like I was dying inside. One day I was in the living room playing when I heard my mother at the door. I dropped everything I was doing and ran to her, jumping in her arms like I did every time. It was like I hadn't seen her in years. All of a sudden I noticed she was with a man. "Don't you remember who this is?" she asked me. When I looked – it was my father. I jumped into his arms and hugged him because with him would be my brother, right? I asked for him. "Where is James?" To my horror they replied, "He's still in Jamaica". Being so young, it never occurred to me how much distance there was between where we were and Jamaica. I felt James would join us soon since my dad was finally with us, "It wouldn't be long now," I thought. That day was a good day. We were almost all together, and my life was coming together. Soon we would all be here and be a family again.

That night, however, was not a good night. The first night my dad slept over is tattooed in my brain as one of the worst experiences of my young life. My aunt's apartment was not big, but we all wanted to sleep under the same roof, so somehow we fit everyone. In the room in which I slept, I was on a twin bed with my dad while Matthew was sharing his bed with Aaron. I woke up to see what was on TV because I heard it going off. Matthew saw I was up and told me he wanted us to do what we always did. My father was literally in the next bed, but my cousin could care less. I knew it was 10 at night because at that very moment the network commercial on channel 5 came on saying, "It's 10 p.m. Do you know where your children are?" At that moment I glanced at my father, hoping he would wake up and save me from this ongoing nightmare. But to my horror, he slept, while his 5 year old daughter was being treated like a street prostitute.

LETS PAUSE FOR A BIT

At this time, I would like to talk to the parents of young children and teens. As I said earlier, one of my reasons for writing this book is to help parents. I do not blame my father for not knowing about what was going on. This is, however, a perfect place to illustrate a point that must be made.

I look at this situation–the first night my father was with me–and in a spiritual way see Christian parents who are asleep while their kids are being molested by the enemy. There are things the enemy could be doing right under your nose and you don't see it. My friends, the enemy does not play fair. He will not wait for our children to be stronger and of age before he worms his way into the home. Too many parents are asleep, or should I say "preoccupied" with life, that they are unaware of the enemy's schemes.

Look at 1 Peter 5:8 –

"Be alert and sober of mind. Your enemy the devil prowls around like a roaring lion looking for someone to devour." (NIV)

According to the *Amplified Bible*, **"Be alert and sober of mind"** means **"Be well balanced."** In today's society, we as parents are anything but well balanced. We are so focused on the demands of this world that our priorities are mixed up. For example, providing for our family financially is good. However, when we are keeping our kids in daycare and school programs, for 10, 12 maybe even 14 hours a day (because we are at the office or even church), when is there time for family bonding? Or when we have our kids in so many extracurricular activities, like sports and clubs, that church becomes secondary. We are not only off-balance, but we collect the materials the enemy uses to build traps our kids fall into. In a very non-intentional way, we teach them that it is not a big deal to miss church.

Believe it or not, even attending church and serving in ministries all the time rather than spending time with your family, **is** a definite opening for the enemy. I have seen the families of many pastors destroyed because the church was more of a priority than their children or spouse. I have seen pastors leave special moments with their families because a church member called in need of something. 1 Timothy 3 gives us a really good guideline for leadership in the church and what it should look like. Verses 4 and 5 say it best:

> *"He must manage his own family well and see that his children obey him, and he must do so in a manner worthy of full respect. (If anyone does not know how to manage his own family, how can he take care of God's church?)" (NIV)*

I remember watching a documentary on *National Geographic* where a pride of lionesses had not eaten for a very long time. They were going after big prey, and because they had not eaten in such a long time they were weak and unable to keep up to kill the large prey. The chase would start, but to no avail, the prey would slip away. One day a herd of buffalo came around with a baby buffalo in their group. The lionesses strategically got into place and chased the mother. You would think they would go after the baby, but they were making the mother **think** she was the target, when actually, the mother was just being pushed away from her baby. They did this so that the head lioness could attack the baby buffalo. I will not forget the scene when the mother buffalo realized her baby was not with her. It was like she forgot for a moment she had a baby. At that moment, she turned around and went looking for her baby. She did not care about the very danger from which she had just been running from. She went back for her baby. To her horror, her baby was surrounded and already wounded. That mother buffalo tried desperately to fight off all the lionesses, but it was too late. Her child had been so fatally wounded she had no other choice but to abandon it and let her baby be devoured by her enemies.

Raising children in this society is hard. It can sometimes pull us in several directions, but we should never sacrifice our families for ministry or anything else. Children don't come with instructions. But we do have the word of God, which has the answers to any question you can think of. There is nothing we can come up with for which the Word is not able to prepare us.

1 Peter 5:8 goes on to say, **"Your enemy the devil prowls around LIKE a roaring lion."** We should have nothing to fear because the One we serve is not **"_like_"** a roaring lion. He **IS** "The Lion of Judah." The enemy wants to bring fear on us, but as you read this, do not be fearful in thinking the enemy will overtake your children. We have a God who is greater than any trap the devil can set before us. But please listen, we have to do our part. You are not running this race

just for yourself. Your family needs you to lay them at the altar every day and seek wisdom for the trials of life they will face. If you need help with that, look to the book of James:

__James 1:5__ : "If any of you lacks wisdom, you should ask God, who gives generously to all without finding fault, and it will be given to you." (NIV)

Lastly, the enemy is **"looking for someone to devour."** As I said in the beginning, he is looking for someone, anyone. And if you think he will attack you first before your children, you are sadly mistaken. I remember watching one of my favorite Bugs Bunny cartoons. Bugs is watching a boxing match when one of the characters in the fight, who was losing, pulls out a pair of glasses. He puts them on and says, "You wouldn't hit a guy with glasses would you?" I've known some parents who think like that when it comes to their children. They think that because we wouldn't fight that dirty and since we are obviously more of a threat than our children, Satan will leave them alone. **<u>ABSOLUTELY NOT</u>**! I believe our kids are hated more than we are. Don't believe me?—read Matthew 18. When Jesus was asked about who was greatest in the kingdom, who did he use as an example? That's right—a child. He looked at the humbleness of that child and told people they pretty much needed to learn from him. Then He really said something interesting. In Matthew 18: 6 Jesus lays down the law:

"If anyone causes one of these little ones—those who believe in me—to stumble, it would be better for them to have a large millstone hung around their neck and to be drowned in the depths of the sea." (NIV)

OUCH!!!!! You can bet there is a target placed on your children by Satan. From the friends who influence them, to the shows they watch and the music they listen to. He will use any device possible to lure them away from hearing God. And that is why Christ said what He said, because it is the parents and those of influence who are to protect them. See, children are trusting by nature (that is what lured me) and God holds us accountable for what we lead them to trust in and do.

Children are a legacy and they are the future. In Exodus, when the children of Israel were increasing in Egypt, who did the Egyptians kill?—The babies. Why? So they could keep the people of God from growing. Someone once told me that "more REAL men and women of God need to have children so they can raise up new warriors for God's Kingdom." She went on to say, "Too many people in church today are defeated and are raising defeated children." That's deep! Satan is playing for keeps, parents. He has no rules and as long as you open or forget to shut some doors, he takes that as an invitation. And he doesn't leave as easily as he came in. (Thanks for letting me vent a little.)

BACK TO THE STORY

How was I going to get out of this mess? How was this all going to end? Well, it wasn't too long before my dad went to live with my mom. I was left to live in this place of disgust and hurt. One fateful day, I was in pre-school and all the kids were waiting for some loving parent, friend or guardian to show up to take them home. I was waiting patiently hoping that my mother or Aaron would pick me up. I felt my heart drop when I heard my name and saw that it was Matthew calling out to me. I slowly got my backpack. I knew what this meant.

We began to walk home and he started off the conversation with, "No one's home. You know what that means." I stayed silent as my throat started to dry up and I felt this pain within me. At that very moment I heard a voice speak to me that I had never heard before. "Don't worry. You will be okay. Aaron is going to come home just before Matthew can do anything to you. He will never do that to you again." When we finally got home we did our normal prepping and just before we started I said, "What if Aaron comes in?" "He won't be home anytime soon," Matthew answered. "No one is supposed to be home for a long time." My heart sank. We were without our clothes, but just before anything happened, in walked Aaron.

My friends, it was all God, because the door to my aunt's apartment is heavy and it slams hard. Hearing the door would have been enough time for Matthew to cover up what we were doing. But it happened just like the voice had said. Aaron screamed and demanded to know what was going on, but we were both in shock. He picked me up, took me out of the room and then closed the door. I don't know what happened behind those closed doors, but I was never to stay there again. Aaron made a phone call, packed all my stuff and walked me to my parents' place. I must say this walk was not an easy walk. It was very long and he never said one thing to me. I thought I had done something wrong because of Aaron's silence. When we finally arrived at my parents' place my dad was there waiting for us. My father must have been the one my cousin called because he knew what had happened. I was confused and didn't understand my dad's anger. My father grabbed my shoulders and started shaking me, "What did he do to you!? Tell me what he did!" I couldn't say anything because I was in such shock; I wasn't expecting him to react that way. I was still in pure shock as he shook me for answers. He turned to Aaron and said, "I'm going to kill him." My dad left the house with my cousin chasing after him screaming and pleading with him. I was left in my parents' apartment as the two of them discussed what happened.

At the age of 5, the damage was done. There was nothing anyone could do about it. I was filled with images and emotions that would not be easily forgotten. And yet no one was brave enough to explain it to me. No one talked to me about it. My mother never said anything to me—my aunt, uncle, dad, Aaron—no one. They never addressed it, they just ignored it.

I would love to tell you that it was all over. I would like to say that since we never spoke of it my world went back – like it never happened. I would love to tell you that God healed me from this one tragic season of my life and that the story ends there. I am sad to say this season of my life was the least of my trials. My molestation was not the demon I was going to fight.

AN UNTREATED WOUND

What naturally happens to a major wound that is ignored and untreated? It gets infected. Isn't it funny how we can get an infection in our finger and our whole body shuts down? Why doesn't the infection stay where the wound is? – Because it's all connected. My wounded soul spread into everything. My parents didn't see it right away, but it was there. If you have ever had the unfortunate experience of either being a parent of someone molested or being molested yourself, you will see this is truly an infection that spreads slowly but dangerously. There needs to be ongoing treatment to cure this infection. There is no quick fix for the innocence of someone who's had it stolen from them, no matter what age.

Unfortunately, if I had to choose between the season of molestation and the upcoming years of abuse I was to endure, I would have chosen the molestation hands down. What I was going to endure has changed me forever.

My parents found a landlord who was willing to rent them a room in his house. When he found out they had a little girl he did not hesitate in welcoming me. I thought living with my parents would be a dream come true, but that changed quickly. I was not the little girl they remembered from 2 years ago. I became very promiscuous. Yes, I was only 5 years old. But I was very aware of sexuality and the way it made me feel and I craved it and sought after it. I became a handful, to say the least, and quickly found trouble if I looked hard enough, which I did. My mouth became very "un-5-year-old like." I started picking up words and phrases that got me slapped around a lot by my father.

We were poor in America and life was hard – even I noticed it. My mother was able to find a job as a "live in nanny" for a family in the rich part of Manhattan. She only came home once or twice a week. Occasionally, she allowed me to spend a night with her at her job. I was quickly able to understand the differences between rich and poor because the house in which she worked was gigantic. The little girl she took care of had everything. Her room was so big that she had a slide in it as well as a play set. She had toys that could put toys stores out of business. There was even a space for her and I to ride two bicycles. All of that was great, but overall, I was just happy I got to be with the person I loved the most, my mom. Life was great with her.

The harsh reality was that she couldn't allow me to stay with her all the time. I couldn't believe that even while living with her she was still leaving me for days at a time. It didn't make any sense to me. I couldn't help but break down in tears each and every time she left. I would literally block the door and rip at her clothes because I didn't want her to leave. I wasn't 2 or 3, I was almost 6 years old doing whatever I could to get her to stay. I had to suck it up each time though, because unlike at my aunt's house, I was not allowed to express my emotions here. I remember one time my mom was leaving and I was begging her to stay, because I knew what it would be like with her gone. It would be bad, really bad.

My father was not the man I remembered back in Jamaica. He was harsh and abusive. One day when my mom went to work I started crying hysterically. Once the door closed, my father came to me and told me to shut up and if I dropped one more tear he would beat me. We went in the kitchen so I could have breakfast. I sat at the table and waited, but I couldn't help it. I tried so hard to hold it in, but tears were still rolling down my eyes. I tried to wipe my tear before he saw it, but it came down just as he looked at me. "Are you still crying?" With utter fear and a lump in my throat I answered, "No." He screamed, "You want to cry, I'll give you something to cry for." He went into the bedroom and I heard him go through the drawers and take out his belt. Fear gripped me and I could not move. He grabbed me by my clothes and beat me so hard I urinated all over myself. He continued to beat me with his thick leather belt until I was on the floor on my knees blocking the blows. Once it was over I looked at the doorknob of the kitchen door and I actually thought to run out the door and find my mother.

A BRIEF THOUGHT ON DISCIPLINE VS ABUSE

I know I have alluded to it, but I have to reiterate that I was a really difficult child to contain and I found myself in a lot of trouble. The more I was abused, the worse I became. The <u>beatings</u>, not spankings, never kept me in line; they did the total opposite. I have heard people use abuse cases like mine to say, "See, that's why I don't spank my kids. Look at what it does to children." Keep this in mind however; this was not a loving father disciplining his child to make her a better person. He was a monster with rage issues and I was the outlet for that rage. He could not control me at the age of five, and as I grew older, he had even less control over me. There was no love shown in his "spankings." I was "ABUSED" never "DISCIPLINED." My father was not sitting me down and warning me, providing a chance to do right. He expected perfection from an imperfect, wounded and confused child. I was a marred piece of clay and he hated what he saw, so I was treated like the dog that doesn't stop going into the garbage. I was physically beaten, called names, not shown love or even given a chance to express my feelings. All these things added up to me growing angrier and more rebellious.

To those who may think spanking can cause a child to be damaged and more messed up, I need to put this out there. There is *Discipline* and there is *Abuse*. You may not agree with me on this point and that is fine. However, though I was abused, God has taught me how to lovingly discipline and correct my own children appropriately. If you are a parent who has adopted spankings as a last result for ongoing offenses, allow God to lead you through His Word and His love. Be sure that your children do not see only the disciplinarian, but that they also see the protector. I did not see a protector, so I feared and began to hate my father. Allow your children the opportunity to be heard, but at the same time help them to understand that misbehavior, disrespect and breaking the rules are not allowed. If you do these things and you lead them in the instruction of the Lord, you'll see your children grow with a healthy balance and respect for you.

Chapter 3

"HE'S GOT THE WHOLE WORLD IN HIS HANDS"

FIRST GRADE

I started a new school not too far from my father's new job as a security officer. I was six years old when I saw that life would be different in 1st grade. It was awkward, because it was here that a new issue began. For some reason (and I can't imagine why) I got into a lot of conflicts with the other kids. Now I know that I had a smart mouth and nasty attitude, but there was this one kid in my class named Michael who would make comments to me that would get me so angry.

One day, shortly after starting school Michael felt it necessary to pound the day lights out of me. I really don't remember what started it all, I just know that as soon as school was over we exchanged words. Then he grabbed me and started beating me up. I had scratches all over. When I walked (oh yes, at six I walked all by myself after school) to my father's office, he was shocked at what he saw. He could not believe how I looked. Even worse was the fact that I let a boy do that to me. It was then my father told me, "If you come here after school and tell me that you let some boy beat you, I'm going to beat you myself. Tomorrow, you are going back to school and you are going to find that boy and beat him."

Now for the sake of those who are reading, I want you to know I am a Christian and because of that I write this book choosing not to write the actual words my father used. My father had, as they say, "The Mouth of a Sailor," so understand that I am censoring his quotes – always. He went on to say it over and over again throughout the day, adding, "When you go back to school you are going to tear that kid up!" He even told me to put rocks in my lunchbox and to beat him with it.

I went back to school and waited until the end of the day to confront Michael, just like he had done to me. Before I even approached him, he was there waiting for me and began running off his mouth. With all my bad behavior, I had never laid my hands on another human being until this day. Now remember, this was not two teenagers, we were two kids who barely knew how to clean ourselves after using the bathroom. I don't remember how it all started, but I remember how it ended. With everything in me, I pinned that boy to the gate and I beat him till I couldn't any longer. I knew it was either him or me. The thought of going home and getting beat was not an option, so I let my frustration out on him because I knew he could take it.

THE CHOICES WE MAKE . . .

Could my behavior have gotten any worse? Yes, it could. And yes, it did. The rage I experienced when punching Michael opened another door. I truly believe that if unchecked, children can inherit the sins of their parents and in some cases have to battle even harder with those "demons." This is why it is so important to understand that it is not just our sins that affect us. Any parent knows this is true if they look closely enough. Children pick up certain habits and traits, good and bad, that at times mimic to the tee, their parents. And it's not just those kids who grow up with parents in the home either. I have known several young people who were raised by single parents or grandparents who were told they behave or share in the same habits as their parents. The possibilities can be endless. The similarities between children and parents can go from a love for a particular flavor of ice cream, to a favorite style of music; Or inheriting a parent's gift of creating art to having a passion for reading. How many of you know, though, that just as good qualities can be inherited, so can bad ones.

I don't have a degree in psychology yet but Scripture is filled with stories showing the sins of the father falling on the children. Look at Abraham. Here we have a wonderful man, and if it was not for him walking in obedience to God by leaving his country, well, that would be pretty much it. At the same time, he made a lot of mistakes his kids and grandchildren repeated, causing great problems for themselves. We know Abraham slept with his wife's slave because Sarah could not have children, but in Genesis 12 and 20, Abraham also lied about Sarah twice claiming that she was solely his sister. He even tries to convince himself that he is not technically lying in Genesis 20:12, 13. You would think Abraham would have told Isaac, his son, about these stories and made sure his son understood the mess it caused him, his wife and those to whom he lied. Instead, Isaac did the same exact thing when he lied about Rebekah and said she was his sister in Genesis 26:7-10. It was not just the lying that was the problem, Scripture points out that in both cases these men did not trust God to protect them. Mind you, Isaac's story happens well after Abraham has proven he is loyal and obedient to God.

Isaac and Rebekah then have twin boys – Esau and Jacob. Isaac shows more favor toward Esau, and Rebekah shows more favor toward Jacob (Genesis 27). This caused a division between Esau and Jacob that continued through generations. Jacob saw the negative effects of these actions. Yet, years later, he favors his son Joseph. This causes a division between Joseph and his ten half-brothers. This ultimately leads to Joseph being sold into slavery in Genesis 37. Let's also not forget that Jacob made the same mistake his grandfather made. He slept with his wives' (he had two) maids which sent the family into a state of chaos (Genesis 30).

Another example is David, the man after God's own heart. He loved God, but he also had a weak spot for the ladies. His lust almost destroyed him and his family when he took wife after wife for himself. He became so greedy that when he saw Bathsheba, another man's wife, he killed her husband after impregnating her (2 Samuel 11-12). That firstborn ends up dying as a result of David's sin. They later have a second son who becomes the next king. He follows in his father's footsteps by taking wife after wife, totaling up to 1000 women according to 1 Kings 11.

The list goes on and on. My friend, I was also walking in the shadow of my parents' sins. I was fighting their demons. I came to find out later that their history with rebellion, lust, violence, rage and much more was reflected in the way I perceived life. I truly believe that the mood and emotions set over a home affect the mood and emotions of all those who live there, especially the children. I don't blame my parents completely, they too were victims of their own past and they tried to live life as best as they could. Besides, I know I have to ultimately take some responsibility for the decisions I made.

Parents who are reading this–who are believers–will understand when I say the following. (Please allow me a moment to emphasize this for you.) God has entrusted you with your children to bring them up according to **His** ways. The sphere of influence you have to help mold them into the adults they need to become for His Kingdom lasts only for a short period of time. Despite what you may think, they are first and foremost God's property. God knows and loves all children before they are even formed in their mother's womb and He has plans for them all.

> ***Jeremiah 1:5 :***
> ***"Before I formed you in the womb I knew you, before you were born I set you apart; I appointed you as a prophet to the nations." (NIV)***

A SEED PLANTED IN ME

Yes, God has a plan for each child, but guess what... so does the devil. The enemy thought he was winning because he had plans for me and it looked like everything was going as planned.

> ***Behold, I will make thee a new sharp threshing instrument. Isaiah 41:15a***

The truth is, before I became "God's new instrument," I was Satan's old instrument. At this point I pray you will have the patience to follow me through this journey of being broken, marred and hurt. Satan thought he had me right where he wanted me. However, just like God used the bad choices made by Abraham, Isaac, and David to show his glory and use their mistakes for His good, God was likewise using my circumstances as a way to develop me into His warrior. Out of all the things He could have used, it was while I was in daycare that God used my secular teachers to plant a seed in me that never left.

He's got the whole world in his hands,
He's got the whole world in his hands,
He's got the whole world in his hands,
He's got the whole world in his hands!

And they would end the song with:

He's got everybody here in his hands,
He's got everybody here in his hands,
He's got everybody here in his hands,
He's got the whole world in his hands!

I was in *"His"* hands? Who was this "He" in whose hands I was in? I didn't know at the time, but I wanted to meet Him. It wasn't until I was much older that I looked back and saw that even then I was in His hands. And when I realized that, I made the promise that no one would ever pluck me out of them.

TO BE A CHILD CLOSE TO JESUS

"Let the little children come to me, and do not hinder
them, for the kingdom of God belongs to such as
these." Mark 10:14 (NIV)

43

To me, the most precious pictures of Jesus are those of Him surrounded by children. Whether it's with them on His lap, carrying one in His arms while another is at His side or even the one where He is placing one on His shoulders, they were all precious to me.

When we think of Jesus, we remember Him healing people, rebuking demons, praying for the will of the Father before going to the cross, or even that moment when He is on the cross all bloody and unrecognizable. Remember though, that Jesus loves children and He had quite a few moments with them while here on earth. What was it like for those precious children to touch Him, to laugh with Him? You can't have an encounter with God, no matter how young or old you are, and not be affected by it. What did those children see in Him that made them want to be around Him and listen? Did Jesus play games with them like "Jewish Hide and Seek" or "Pin The Tail on the Master's Donkey?" How can you have kids around you and not play games? Did they blindfold Jesus, poke Him and pull at the hem of His garment for fun to see if He would catch them or call out the name of the child who touched him?

I wonder if Jesus looked at each child and if He knew what they had been through and what they were going to go through? Were some going to lose their parents way too early? Were some going to be targets of the enemy? Did he hold some closer than others or hold on to one longer than the others because he saw moments of discouragement and fear in their future? One can only ponder. I would have done anything to be one of those kids, but I wasn't.

I found myself in many altercations with my classmates after that incident with Michael. Most of my worries were of my father beating me if he found out I did not defend myself. Many years later my mother told me things started getting really bad for me in school and my teacher called her. She told my mom she was very concerned because I was such an aggressive child. My teacher was so concerned that she sat down one day and asked me why I was getting into so many fights. I remembered that time as my mom told the story. My teacher asked, "What is it you want," and I replied, "I just want my mother." What I didn't know was my teacher spoke with my mother about the possibilities of changing jobs because her absence was affecting me.

It wasn't long after that my parents moved to their own place. This time it was an apartment and not just a room. In addition, my mother was no longer working as a live-in nanny. She was now a babysitter and coming home every day. She would read books to me at nights when she could. And she would even cook dinner sometimes. But due to her hours, I was still with my father more than I was with her.

I remember being in my room and taking out a book as I began to imitate her reading to me. I absolutely loved *Sesame Street* and my favorite character of all was Grover. One of my favorite story books was about Grover being afraid because he heard that a monster was in the book, but he didn't realize he was the monster. The book was called, *"Monster at the End of This Book."* I really wanted to read it, but I could not read all the words. It was read to me enough that I began to memorize the story page for page. Wherever I didn't really remember the exact words I started to make up the story, as most five or six year olds would. All of a sudden, from the other room, my father called to me and said to come to his room and to bring the book. "I want you to read to me," he said. That was enough to cause real fear to set in, but I started to read. When I came to a word and read it wrong he made me stop and sound it out. It all started off fine, but when I kept reading he got frustrated with me and said, "Is that what it says?" He had a look in his eyes. I knew it meant if I didn't get this word right, he was going to beat me. I didn't know the word, so he grabbed his leather belt and told me to try again, as if threatening me was going to help. I was so afraid and just could not do it. This was one of the most traumatic beatings, because it was one that would not end. He put me in front of the book again and told me what the word was. Then he had me start to read it over again. If I forgot the word or came to another word I did not know the beating continued. Tears come to my eyes even now as I write this to you. The beating only stopped when my mother came home from work. I was so thankful for those moments. On this day, she noticed something wrong and asked what was going on. My father didn't really have an answer, he just looked at me and I looked at her with tears running down my face. My father dismissed me and I ran to my room. A few minutes later she came into my room and asked me to lift up my shirt. She started looking at my back and began to run her fingers over the welts the belt left behind. It was an awkward moment, my mother made no apology or explanations for him, she just covered me and left.

As time went on, my hate for my father grew, and it appeared to me that his hate for me grew as well. He never showed me any kind of affection. My father never touched me unless he was beating me. He cursed at me more than he praised me. The thing I know for sure is that he wanted no one putting their hands on me. It was weird to me, because my father was very protective over me when it came to other people and he always provided for all my physical needs. Those acts were the only proof I had of his love for me. In my older years, I found out about his past and had a better understanding of the term "hurting people hurt people." If God is the true embodiment of love, can a person who does not know Him ever really give love? It is a question of debate. What I know is that my father was a hurting man. He was consumed by his own battles of resentment, unforgiveness and bitterness and it was reflected back in his own parenting.

LIFE CHANGES AND STILL NO JAMES

My mother was home more but because of her work hours she was always so tired. My father would take me to the park or out to ride my bike so she could get some rest.

Her life was wearing her down and I later understood why. Both my parents had their hearts and minds on getting James, here to the states with us, but it wasn't working out as either of them had expected. I heard her say many times James was coming, but years went by and nothing happened. Christmas after Christmas, I was told he would be with us, but the holidays would come and he was still in Jamaica.

I remember one Christmas season my mother brought me to Macy's and we stood on line so I could sit on Santa's lap. This was the one and only time I ever did this. When I finally got the chance to see this great, mysterious, all-powerful figure, I had one request only, "I would like you to bring my brother to me. He is away in Jamaica and I want him with me." Santa looked at me and then looked at my mother and said he would try his best. To my surprise, my brother did not join us as I expected – so much for Santa. I know now what was going on, but back then I could not understand the turmoil my parents were feeling.

In the midst of it all, God saw fit to allow my mother to get pregnant with my younger brother Peter. For me, that was the best news I had heard in a long time. I was so excited I wanted to tell everyone. The thought of a little brother made me feel like I would always have someone to be with. He wasn't the only change in my life. One summer day, my dad was outside talking to a few of his friends as I was playing. He then called me over and said, "This is Mr. and Mrs. Anderson. They want to know if you would like to go to Sunday School with them. What do you think of that?" My immediate thought was, "School? Who would want to go to school on a Sunday?" In my head I said, "No," but with my mouth I said, "Yes. I would like to try it." Where did that come from? Well, that unexpected "Yes" changed my life. The following Sunday, Mr. and Mrs. Anderson picked me up, like they said, and it was one of the best days I had in my life.

Psalms 71:20, 21
"Though you have made me see troubles,
many and bitter,
you will restore my life again;
from the depths of the earth
you will again bring me up.
You will increase my honor
and comfort me once more." (NIV)

I didn't know it at the time, but God was setting me on a path that would ultimately restore all the enemy thought he had stolen from me. My parents did not join us on Sundays, and I know this is bad, but I was so happy. I finally felt I was able to have some freedom. The people there were absolutely the nicest people I had ever met. There was a little class for kids my age and there was a teacher. Once the class was over I found Mrs. Anderson. We sat in the balcony and there were maroon colored books everyone sang from. Then there was a man all the way down stairs talking to everyone. The cool thing was they had breakfast for everyone, some grape juice in a very small plastic cup and thin little crackers. I was only allowed one cracker and when the man down on stage told us, we broke it and then ate it (this was communion if you hadn't guessed). I have no idea what he was talking about, but I eventually thought it was time for a nap. They woke me up when it was all over and then we went back in the car.

Obviously, I did not come out quoting scripture and saved. The only thing I remembered was Mr. and Mrs. Anderson and the loving and caring nature they had towards me.

With them, something else became clear to me. The love they had for their daughter, Renee, who was almost two, gave me a glimpse of what I was missing with my father. It was the first time I realized that maybe what my father was doing to me was not normal. Renee was a hyper girl, and so was I, but we were having fun with each other. In the car heading home after the church service we were loud, but her dad never cursed or slapped her. He answered her with love and she jumped in his arms whenever she could. When they had to, they disciplined her with love. WHAT WAS THAT!?!?! I did not understand that! That's why it was so painful to come back into my home. I could feel the oppression and the gloom. It was the atmosphere the Andersons gave off that made me feel something I never felt before, and that made me go back to church the next week and every week after that.

YES, ANOTHER QUICK PAUSE

If there is ever someone to whom you are trying to witness, can I just tell you it's not just the words you preach or the scriptures you share. It's the love of Christ, the love that surpasses all else that makes a difference. Look at what Jesus says:

> *"A new command I give you: Love one another. As I have loved you, so you must love one another. By this everyone will know that you are my disciples, if you love one another."* **John 13:34-35 (NIV)**

The way we show love is how we draw in those who are in the world. Some think you must beat them in the head with Scripture or condemn them for not knowing the truth. We are to love them in the dirt and show them they are valued by God. The more truth an unbeliever is shown about Christ the more they become uncomfortable with the life they are living. We, as God's people, must love each other as well. Sometimes we are the worst example to the world as we tear each other down and fight back and forth in the church. Why would anyone want to leave a world of fighting, backbiting, and betrayal for another world full of the same thing, if not worse?

Church became my safe haven and I grew to love the Andersons more and more, but I was soon going to be challenged with the things I was hearing on Sundays.

Chapter 4

GOD?

NO TIME TO BE A CHILD

As I continued going to church I heard a great deal about this God in Heaven, but I never took him home with me. Was I supposed to believe that there was this invisible being who created us all and loved us? He created the whole world and wanted a relationship with us, but He never spoke or even introduced himself? On top of that, if we did not accept this God into our lives we couldn't go to this place called "Heaven", the place where God lived. Instead, we would go to this other place called "Hell," where it was really hot and where only bad people went. I personally thought if bad people were there we wouldn't have to be good—we could be as bad as we wanted and not get in trouble. Hell didn't sound as bad as they were trying to make it.

I heard this every Sunday for a year but for some reason I never thought about it when I went home. I was not interested in this God. I was not interested in reading about the fairy-tales. I already had Sesame Street.

Life at home was not getting any better. I was seven when my brother was finally born. His birth was one of the happiest days of my life. With him here, I now had someone to be with and to play with, even though it would be a while before he could really play along. My mother did not have an easy delivery so she had to return to the hospital for a time. While she was there, I stayed with my Aunt Suzy. I was eager to help with my new baby brother. My Aunt even told my mother she barely needed to do anything because I was so good at taking care of Peter.

My mother had to return to work as soon as she was able. When she did, the new routine was that while my father slept early in the morning, my mother would wake me up to take care of Peter for a few hours. When I got home from school, my dad would give me something to eat and then leave me to take care of Peter . As intense as this may sound to some, taking care of my little brother is what gave me a desire to go home. Honestly, thinking about it now, for a while, that was the only thing that gave me joy. He put a smile on my face and showed me unconditional love; He was happy when I was with him. I did start to grow jealous of him, though. All of the attention was now on Peter , and I understood why, so it did not bother me. What bothered me was the type of attention he received.

My parents showed Peter a great amount of love, while I was treated more like the hired hand. I never experienced the same form of care and compassion that was given to him. "Why was he so different? Why did he get the kisses and hugs while I was cursed at and beaten?" My mom would come home from work and have no time for me. She took Peter from me and headed straight into her room. It was shortly after he was born that the stories at bedtime ended. Any attempt I made to get attention was seen as me being in the way. In fact, within time, my parents' patience with me lessened, bringing a great increase in beatings. That is how warped I saw things. I was craving attention so much that I would do whatever I could to get it, even if it was negative.

One day, Brother and Sister Anderson called to find out if I was going to church that week. My mother must have become truly desperate, because she stayed on the phone with them complaining about my behavior. My mother handed me the phone. "Hello Sweetie," It was Sister Anderson, "Your mom tells me that you have been acting up. She said you're not listening. Why?" I was silent on the phone as tears ran down my cheek. My parents had never involved others in my behavioral issues before. I didn't know what to say. How could I explain the pain that just wouldn't go away? How could I explain the need for love? I wanted to tell her to pick me up and never bring me back home after church on Sunday, to keep me with her. I couldn't explain myself because what child could at the age of seven, especially with all I was battling with in my head? How could I express all those emotions and then be expected to verbalize them? I could not provide Sister Anderson any answers to her questions, just silence and the sound of sniffles. Then she muttered eight simple words, "Jesus loves you sweetheart, and so do we."

SAME TROUBLE, DIFFERENT FORM

After that day, I really did try to do things right but it would just not turn out the way I wanted. I found myself the focus of the bullies in school. I tried becoming invisible to avoid trouble, but the other kids took my quietness as a form of weakness. I really cannot recall how they knew, but some of them found out about the abuse I received at home. That information is what they used to make fun of me and provoke me. This, in my eyes, gave me good reason to defend myself. However, choosing to fight meant I must win or I would have to face my father. Fighting also meant getting into trouble at school, which meant a phone call home, which meant another beating. I was constantly picked on by the kids in school, most of the time from the boys. There were days when I was able to resist fighting back, deciding to take the insults and move on. Other days, however, I could not take it. I would let my fists do all the talking. If fighting was the only "curse" that haunted me that might have been fine. But another haunting pain from my past was going to reveal its head. This time, however, it would take on a new form.

It started because my father needed to find a babysitter for my brother and me after school while he worked. He was able to find one with the help of an older gentleman named Mr. Pike who lived in the same building where my father worked. Mr. Pike had a granddaughter, Kelly, who attended the same school as I. She was about ten or eleven years old. She was told to wait for me after school so we could go to her grandfather's house together. My father made sure to tell them that if I did not listen to them they were to let him know and he would deal with me afterward.

In the beginning, everything was fine, but surprisingly Kelly asked me to do sexual things with her. When I resisted her, she threatened to tell my father I was not listening. It felt like I was back in the same situation with Matthew all over again. I remembered how scared I was of my father back then, as if it was my fault. The last thing I wanted was to get into trouble again. I did whatever she told me to do. On a few occasions, Kelly would beat on me, and I had to let her do what she wanted. She knew how to control me, instilling fear every single time. I have no words to describe how it felt except that it was "evil." The combination of her physical and sexual abuse, along with the added fear of her saying to me, "You know they won't believe you. Your dad is just going to beat you!" had my mind so clouded that to this day I am not able to put that moment into words adequately. I had hoped each time that Mr. Pike would walk in, but he was never around, so it would have been her word against mine.

I was fighting in school, I was molested and beaten by my babysitter, I was ignored and beaten at home, and why? I did not know. I realize some of you reading this may have a very difficult time believing my story. The thought that these experiences could happen to such a young girl here in America with no one noticing is impossible. I mean, the girl molesting me was only a child herself. No child that age forces another to do things so horrific. How could all that bullying go on, and for so long in a public school without raising any attention? I am unable to provide for you a reasonable answer. I would question these things myself, if not for the fact that I am the one who lived through it. Let me remind you that even though this may seem a bit much, it is still only a portion of what really went on.

One winter day, my parents bought me a new hat and pair of gloves. They told me not to forget them at school. At the end of one school day, Kelly came to my class to pick me up and walk me home. She was rushing me and I couldn't find my hat.

"I can't find my hat!!" I said frantically.

"You'll get it tomorrow. Let's go!" she yelled from the door.

"No, I have to get it now or I'll get in trouble," I replied.

"I'm leaving now and I'm telling your father you didn't listen to me," was her answer.

I had to make the choice to leave without the hat. When we got to Kelly's house we put our stuff down and had a snack. There was a little playground right downstairs from her building so she asked me if I wanted to go outside. I told her I didn't want to because I didn't have my hat. Kelly told me if I didn't listen she would beat me up again and then tell my dad. I went outside and just as I envisioned it, my father came around the corner ten minutes later and saw me playing without the hat. He called me over and asked me where my hat was. Before I could tell him what happened he dragged me to the corner of the building and took off his belt and started beating me in public. I had never been so humiliated. The other kids watched as he beat me on my head and face in the cold. My father was the security officer for that area so no one stopped him. Why was this happening to me again? Because I left my hat in school? The punishment definitely did not fit the crime.

When we arrived home my father finally asked me what happened.

"Really? Now? After all that, you want to ask that question now?" I thought to myself.

Instead, I said to him, "Kelly has been beating me up almost every day." I could not bring myself to tell him about the sexual things because I remembered how he screamed at me when he found out what Matthew had done. I continued explaining why I didn't have my hat on and mentioned to him that I was scared of Kelly. I lifted up my shirt to show him a scratch she had given me to prove I was not lying. My father had gone nuts on me, but I had never seen him so angry. And this time his anger was not directed at me. He lost it. He dropped my brother off somewhere and together we went back to Kelly's house that day. My father banged on Mr. Pike's apartment door demanding that Kelly come out into the hallway. My dad had all intentions of beating her up. My father was not threatening to do this, he was truly going to do this. Mr. Pike told my father if he did not leave he was going to call the cops. My father did leave, but not before expressing some choice words I cannot repeat. I never saw Kelly again, not even in school.

Unfortunately, though that nightmare was over, my school problems were not. In fact, now that some kids had seen firsthand how my father would beat me, the laughter and bullying at school increased. I felt forced to resolve issues with my fists and I am not proud of it. I was constantly being mocked by the members of my class. I was angry. One day we were in class and I tried to defend my father's actions by saying he did it because he loved me. I knew I only said it to convince myself that it was true.

Sometime shortly after the rumors began, my father was called into school because of my behavior. My father, my teacher and I spoke out in the hallway while the class continued their work. My teacher explained that I had been talkative and fresh. She went on to say I was careless and not focused. (Are you saying "uh-oh" as you read this yet?) She mentioned that I was constantly hurting myself and I needed to get myself together. Lastly, as if she was doing me a favor, she used that great teacher's voice of encouragement to say, "I know she can do better." And then she left me to talk alone with my dad (smart lady).

As soon as she left, my father began scolding me under his breath and then proceeded to slap me multiple times in the face. I did not know it could be heard in the classroom, but afterwards when I went back in, all eyes were on me. I didn't think they heard anything, but I was wrong, they heard the slapping. The teacher finished what she was saying to the class and then called me over to her desk. She asked if my father had hit me in my face. With tears streaming down my face, I lied and told her "no." My face was visibly swollen on one side and his hand prints were clearly visible. She asked again, but I stood by my answer even though I felt my face swelling as we were speaking. She sent me back to my desk. I put my head down, cried and went to sleep till it was time to go home. Again, I was humiliated.

OUR FIRST CONVERSATION

The only time I could find peace was in church. I continued to go whenever I could. As I grew a little older I heard more teachings about giving God your heart. "Let Him rule your life," they would say. I would listen, but I really wondered when the story would just be over so we could have snacks. That church handed out some delicious snacks. I went home that day, took off my Sunday dress and started playing with my dolls. Church that day was pretty good and I thought it was done, but apparently it was not.

For some of you reading this what I am about to tell you may be hard to believe. I guess you'll just have to make that decision for yourself.

While on the floor in that tiny room, all of a sudden I heard a voice say my name. The voice proceeded to say, "When are you going to give your heart to me?"

I looked around for a moment to see where it came from. No one was in the room, but I answered anyway, "Who are you?"

"God," the voice replied. "When are you going to give your heart to me?" He asked softly and gently.

I was confused. Was this the God I had been hearing about in Sunday school? I hadn't really thought about an answer to His question before. It was honestly never my desire to serve this God.

"I don't know when, but maybe when I'm 30."

It is beyond me why I said 30. I almost feel like he laughed when I said that.

"Why at 30?" He continued.

"Because then I can live my life. I can do what I want and I'll have no one who can tell me what to do, then I'll give my life to you." Then at that moment, I became the one with the comments and questions for Him. "I heard that you are a father. I don't need another parent. I already have two, I don't want a third. If you're such a good God, why would you put me into this family anyway? Why can't you stop my dad from beating me? You can't be that good if you let my father do this to me."

"But what if you die before you are 30? You won't get into Heaven."

He never said anything about my father, and never addressed the questions about me being abused.

"Yes I will go to heaven!" I replied very nasty like. "You have to let me in!"

"Why?" He asked.

"Because I am a little girl and you have to let me in."

At this point, I am almost sure you are questioning this whole situation. Let me explain that this experience with God was not so strange to me because I would walk into a room and see my mother muttering to herself. I would ask her who she was talking to, and she would always reply that she was talking to God. From that point, on every time I saw her doing this I asked if she was talking to God and she would say, "Yes." So, this experience was not scary or uncommon to me, because my mom talked out loud to "God" all the time. I thought, "Oh, now He is talking to me." It wasn't until I was older that she confessed to me she was never talking to God, but to herself, and that she made it up so that I wouldn't think she was weird. However, I was talking to Him.

"No I don't." He said. "Only those who have given me their hearts will enter into heaven."

"Well if you don't let me in, I'll just tell your daddy and mommy on you," I said.

"I don't have a daddy or a mommy," He responded.

"Yes you do. Everyone has a daddy and a mommy. If you don't then who made you?"

I couldn't understand that part at all. At that very moment my whole room went dark and all around me were stars. It was as if I was traveling at super speed into an abyss.

"No one made me. See, I was here from the very beginning and I will be here at the very end. I do love you. But if you don't give your life to me, you will not make it to 30. And only those who love me will enter Heaven."

I will tell you, God never ever spoke to me about Hell, but at the end of it all I had a sense of fear. I believed this God and I knew He was real but the idea of something out there, greater than anyone else–that bothered me. Though I knew He was real, I did not give my life over to Him because I was too scared to live my life with more rules.

God did not stop speaking to me because I didn't receive his offer. I had a few conversations with Him, but this one is the most memorable. Some people have questioned how God could speak to me even when I was not saved. But remember Abraham was not serving the Lord when God called him out of the land of his father. Jacob was a swindler when he had a dream of the ladder reaching to Heaven, and he did not serve the Lord after that remarkable dream. Moses was not serving the Lord when God appeared at the burning bush. Our Lord longs to have relationships with his children.

Let's look again at Mark 10:13 – 16:

"People were bringing little children to Jesus for him to place his hands on them, but the disciples rebuked them. When Jesus saw this, he was indignant. He said to them, 'Let the little children come to me, and do not hinder them, for the kingdom of God belongs to such as these. Truly I tell you, anyone who will not receive the kingdom of God like a little child will never enter it.' And He took the children in His arms, placed His hands on them and blessed them." (NIV)

The disciples didn't think much of the children. They felt their master was too busy for these annoying, loud, snot-nosed little brats. But Jesus saw them differently. He rebuked the disciples! Would Jesus have to rebuke you? Do you see every child, no matter how annoying, the way Jesus did? He felt the kingdom of God belonged to children and those like them. He doesn't expect us to be childish or naïve, but He finds their innocence, faith, meekness and pureness of heart to be perfect attributes for those who would reign with Him one day.

The Scriptures go on to say that Jesus took them in His arms and blessed them. What do you think that was like? Oh man! The thought of being in the arms of Jesus during that painful time of my life brings a lump to my throat. I didn't realize I *was* in His arms at the time, but I know now. They were invisible arms to the naked eye, but those powerful carpenter arms were scooping up all the pieces to my broken puzzle. He was giving me the perfect amount of affection.

Jesus knew every single challenge each child would face. He knew about the hurt and pains–He knew if they were abused like me. He saw into their future, then prayed the perfect prayer and blessed them.

Mark records how the parents brought their children to Jesus. That was not how my story progressed; instead Jesus found another way to come to me. Look, I don't know where you stand on the whole "God Thing," but I realize that not everyone who reads this book may be a believer. You may say to yourself, "God has never shown me that He is real." You may question why your world is what it is. I believe He has given me this opportunity to tell you this . . . GOD IS REAL and HE LOVES YOU!!!!! He has allowed me to set aside months to put this book together as I still go about my day to day life as a mother, wife, ministry leader, student, and Bible Study teacher. Who does that? Between my studies and everything else, I don't have time to write a book–let alone one about my past, that I would much prefer to leave in the past. Yet, somehow, God has lengthened my days, while taking nothing away to allow me the opportunity of reaching out to you. He does not have to be in a burning bush or giant fish to tell you who He is. Sometimes He uses the simplest things, like a book, to do it. That's the kind of God I serve.

I wanted to share these experiences with others and so I did. I told people I was talking to God and that He spoke back. They didn't believe me. Do you know what was worse? Even those from church, my Sunday School teachers, didn't believe me. Thank God that even at that age I didn't care about what people thought of me. Whether they believed me or not, I knew the truth. Christ spoke to me. No one, not even my father could take that away from me.

Chapter 5

NOT AS EASY AS YOU WOULD THINK

"The LORD appeared to us in the past, saying:
"I have loved you with an everlasting love;
I have drawn you with unfailing kindness.
I will build you up again,
and you, Virgin Israel, will be rebuilt.
Again you will take up your timbrels
and go out to dance with the joyful"'
Jeremiah 31:3, (NIV)

WE FALL TO LEARN HOW TO GET BACK UP AGAIN

At the age of eight, I went to church faithfully and I thought a bit more of trying to be a Christian. However, no one ever really taught me what that meant. I needed someone to teach me that if I used bad language once, it didn't mean I would be thrown out on the curb by God. He was more patient than that. I needed to know if I fell short of His grace, whatever that term meant, He only expected me to get up and try again. In Proverbs 24:16 it says: *"though the righteous fall seven times, they rise again . . ."* (NIV)

The problem was that no one told me about the *"rise"* part. All I was taught was how when we sin we make God unhappy. Everything was about creating the fear of not disappointing God, but I was never taught about His forgiveness. HELLO!!!! That part is just as important as the knowledge of sin.

I understand now that my Sunday School teachers were not expecting to have to teach lessons about sin to an 8 year old the way I needed it taught. My battle was not with making my bed or finishing my homework–well it was, but that was nothing compared to my sin. My thoughts were impure, evil and warped. I am older now, but I could never repeat the things I struggled with in their rawest form because this book would be too distasteful. My needs were not being met because I was not like those in the class. I was fighting an adult battle, and I was losing fast.

If you are struggling with things that are not easy to give up, let me talk to you right now. Here's what I wish someone had told me. The chains of sin are real and nothing can break them except Jesus Christ himself. You can't break them and there is no key. It is the hands of God that set you free. God is patient, loving and kind during the whole process.

Let's look at our heart and mind like a computer that has been corrupted with a virus. This virus is programmed to counteract, contaminate and cause us to behave in a way that is different from the way we are designed. When God created Adam, it was to have a relationship with him. When sin came– it was like the virus. We were created in God's image so anything that is different from God will counteract and even try to kill and destroy us. We were never created to be selfish, angry, sexually immoral, unforgiving, or wicked. These things were not part of our original programming. Jesus, knowing this, has come to help us be reprogrammed. We have to be rebooted, cleaned out and have new software installed.

There are those who are able to make a complete 180 degree turn once they give their lives over to the Lord, but there are others who find it a battle leaving the life they had before. I think it is unfair to compare ourselves to others. For one thing, they don't share our lives even if they are in the same home as we. Personalities, views, and emotions are all different. For that reason, I thank the Lord that Jesus does not relate to all of us in the same ways man does. My suggestion is not to walk away from God because of your constant failures. Instead, why not give Him twice the amount of time to "reboot" you. Allow Him the ability to clean out and take apart your "hardware," and find the cause of what is going against the original programming. A virus enters a computer in a matter of seconds and can spread throughout the whole system. In order to clean it out properly one must do it slowly and meticulously to make sure it won't come back or damage the computer beyond repair.

The same goes for the sin we face. It can take time for some of us to be completely cleaned of the temptations and struggles that have haunted us through the years. In fact, I believe at times the longer we have been affected the harder it may be to clean out. Not in all cases, but in many.

There were many times I tried to do what was right in my own strength, but I still found myself in trouble. I got into fights, cursed, you name it–I did it. I felt like once I gave into sin I was dirty all over again and I had lost my chance with God. I expected Him to treat me the same way those around me had. I didn't understand that no one could love me in a way that would mirror His love for me. I was taught to pray for forgiveness and was told that once I did I was forgiven. But then I was told not to do it anymore.... Okay... How??? How do I not do what I have always done? What do I do instead?

How many of you have had times when you felt like a broken record, constantly telling God you were sorry for what you did, but still doing it over and over again? Come on, I know I'm not the only one. You know that doing the same thing over and over again won't produce a different result. I didn't know how to do things differently, so my results were always the same. No one told me about walking in faith and about a constant prayer life. They told me when I did wrong that I was a sinner. But they didn't tell me how to become stronger, or that the journey was going to take a lifetime to walk.

SAME BATTLES, NEW LEVELS

One school day, my father told me my teacher would be giving me a bus pass and that I was not to lose it. That same day, I made a friend by the name of Michelle. She had always been a nasty girl who at times was really cruel and mean, but for some reason she befriended me (go figure). In our times of talking she asked me if the rumors were true about my dad. I opened up to her. I told her everything my dad had done to me and how he whipped me regularly. I shared with her about the growing demands at home of taking care of my brother. Eventually, I started crying because she was the first person I had shared with. It felt good to finally tell someone what I going through. She was mortified and wanted to tell a teacher what was going on, but I begged her not to, so she listened.

When I got home my father immediately asked me for the bus pass the teacher gave me. With all that happened with Michelle, I had totally forgotten I was supposed to get it. I told him the teacher didn't give me a bus pass. "Yes she did and you better find it," he said. I went into my room and looked frantically in my pockets and in the slots of my book bag, but I knew she had not given me anything. He beat me again for losing the bus pass. When my mother came home she went through my bag and there was the bus pass stapled in my notebook with a note attached. My father muttered a flimsy apology as he walked away looking at it.

My father would usually use his thick leather belt and strike me with everything he could out of pure anger. This day, he whipped the belt so hard that one of the strikes caught me across my neck. When he yanked it back it stripped off a piece of skin. Like many times before, my back was so sore I could not sleep comfortably for days. The next day I wore a turtleneck. I thought it would cover up the mark, but it was sticking out and Michelle saw it immediately. She asked me what had happened but I didn't want to say anything right there in class. I took her to the bathroom and lifted up my shirt. She couldn't believe it when she saw the welts all over my back. She started crying because it was too much for her. When we went back to the classroom the teacher asked Michelle why she was crying. I could tell Michelle was going to tell her everything. I grabbed the teacher's arm and told her nothing was wrong.

I was so thankful Michelle cared for me. It made me feel good knowing someone sympathized with me and that I could confide in her. You can imagine then how broken I felt when Michelle told everyone what had happened. I found out she was only befriending me to get information. She had no intention of being my friend. I felt so betrayed. I thought it was one of the cruelest things anyone could do to me. If I wasn't the laughing stock of the school before, I definitely was now.

That was enough for me. I was tired of everything. Tired of the beatings and tired of being bullied. I was tired of the girls threatening to beat me up if I did not meet them in the bathroom to do the unthinkable. Michelle hurt me. It was time for me to let loose. I didn't care anymore. I didn't care if I got in trouble. I didn't care if I won the fight or lost. I was not letting EVERYONE walk all over me any longer.

The first one I wanted to deal with was Michelle. Shortly after I found out she was not a real friend, the teacher lined us all up for the bathroom. When the girls went into the bathroom Michelle started teasing me and making comments about my father. All the girls gathered around to join in. I stepped up to her face and without thinking I slapped her. We fought until the teacher broke it up. I was hurt and I took it all out on her.

As if I didn't have a big enough target on my back, at eight years old I also began to wear glasses, (which I thought was cool). One afternoon after school a boy who had bullied me from the beginning saw me walking to my dad's office and followed me along with two other boys. When I noticed them, I stopped and asked him what he wanted. He just looked at me and started laughing at my glasses. Before I knew it, he slapped my glasses off my face into a ditch and then walked away with his friends laughing. I stood there looking at the glasses and decided to go in the ditch and get them. I put them in my book bag. Then instead of going towards my father's office, which was a minute away, I followed the boys.

One of the friends saw me coming and said, "Hey look who it is."

"Oh you want more?" he asked with a smirk.

"Let's do this," I replied with tears streaming down my face.

He took off his book bag and I stayed there waiting for him to drop it. "Aren't you going to take your book bag off?" asked one of the other guys. I didn't answer. I was going to beat this kid with my coat and my book bag full and on. The third boy, who had stayed silent this whole time, saw the look in my eyes and said, "I don't know if you want to mess with her man. Her dad is crazy, remember?" "Please," the bully said arrogantly, "Her dad can't touch me. I'm gonna be done with her in a minute." The moment he finished that sentence I jumped on him, pulled his coat over his head, pinned him against the car and let my rage out on him. I was not going to stop until I had to.

A man driving in his car saw us and yelled, "Stop that right now!" Then he yelled to the bully, who was still getting himself together, "You shouldn't be fighting a girl. Now you guys go home." Completely humiliated, he picked up his things and continued on his way with the other two boys. I waited until the man left and followed after the boys. "Let's finish this!" I said with all my adrenaline pumping. I knew he would come back again the next day and the day after that. He was not going to leave me alone because I got a few good punches in. I needed to finish this today. I jumped on him a second time and beat him till I was tired. When it was all over, the third boy said, "I told you not to mess with her." That was the last time that bully ever bothered me.

My problem was that he wasn't the only boy who picked on me. There was another boy named Danny who bullied me day in and day out. One day he punched me in the stomach after school. I was going to leave it alone, but my father happened to be in front of my school to take me home. He asked me what happened and I told him one of the boys in my class just punched me in the stomach. He told me to point him out and that's exactly what I did. He told me to stay where I was and he calmly brought the boy to me. "Is this the boy?" he asked. Danny was so nervous and scared. "Did you punch my daughter in the stomach?" Danny started defending himself. Before he could finish what he was saying, my father turned to me and said, "Beat him right now!" Without a second passing, I jumped on Danny and I did to him what I thought would please my father. That poor kid didn't have a chance. With each punch my rage was increasing and I was not trying to stop it. My father finally said just one word and I was done.

From that day on, where I once was a victim of bullying, I was now the bully. I felt that feeling of release as I got out all my frustrations and anger. I picked fights with people I knew I could beat just so I could let loose. I was no longer defending myself, I was now the aggressor. Sometimes I won, sometimes I lost, but it got to the point where it wasn't about winning or losing, it was about feeding my anger. I took out on them what I wished I could do to my father. One of the saddest moments of my childhood was when I started getting known for my fighting and my short fuse. I was one of the smallest kids in my class, so it was a big deal for me to overtake someone. A new girl, by the name of Annie, started at the school and she was pretty tall. During lunch time, when all the kids were joking around she made a joke about me. I didn't care, I even laughed. But because I had a rep for a short fuse they expected a fight. The whole class pressured me to fight Annie after school.

Annie was given a rundown of my reputation, and it was quite clear she wanted no trouble. She didn't want to have to fight one of the toughest kids in the class. Annie apologized and said she was sorry. I really forgave her because I knew she meant nothing by it, but what would happen if I let her go? Would they think I was going soft again? Annie was new. Did she think she could say things like that and get away with it? Would other kids start to bully me again? I sized her up–she was huge and could have easily taken me down if she knew her power. I made up my mind to leave, go home and just forget it. As we were about to walk out of the class to line up she asked me with real fear, "Are you really going to fight me? I did say that I was sorry." "No, I'm not," I reassured her.

As we left school, everyone started chanting for a fight. I looked in her face and saw real fear. But I kept thinking of my pride and rep, so before I knew it I gave into it. I grabbed her by the top of her shirt, pulled her down, socked her in the face and just started pounding on her. I saw her face during the fight and knew this was not right. I know the feeling of fear and wanting mercy–I didn't want to be like this. What was I doing? I was so embarrassed with myself. This was not fair, even if she was big enough to take it. No one had to take me off her, I willingly got off. I started walking away towards home when someone said, "Is that all? You're going to go soft on her?" They wanted more? What more could they have asked for? I taught her a lesson, but I guess not enough to keep up my rep. I had to keep with the rep, so I actually walked back to her and proceeded to hit her all over again.

I was ashamed of myself. To this day I am embarrassed by my behavior. When I went to school the next day Annie was not there. Apparently she never went home after the fight, she had run away from home. Was I really the reason she was missing? What would I do if something actually happened to her? The very kids that egged me on were the same ones who blamed me for her running away. She was found 24 hours later. When she returned to school, I asked her if she was okay. She said, "I ran away from home because of you." Annie was too embarrassed to tell her family what had happened in school, but she made sure to tell me. After that day, she became the one they all started picking on. I tried not to join in, but there were those moments when I did side with the crowd just so I would still be respected.

What kind of person was I becoming? It wasn't just fighting either. I was stealing money from my dad, lying, and slowly becoming addicted to porn. Kids were bringing dirty magazines to school and we would look at them. There were a lot of things that happened in this school that would be considered unbelievable. All I cared about was feeling like I was part of the group, I didn't care about the consequences.

Not too long after, I was given the news that Brother and Sister Anderson were moving away and that they would no longer be able to take me to church. In the four years of going to church with them they also picked up a few others in their larger-than-life station wagon. What was even more wonderful was that the Andersons had told the church leaders all about those they would bring to church. It took a few months to get it going, but the church soon started a van service that would pick me up, as well as the others who carpooled with Mr. and Mrs. Anderson every Sunday.

Despite how the rest of my week was, I looked forward to Sunday mornings. It was the one day of the week I was leaving my world and traveling to another one. The truth remained that I still didn't believe half the stuff I heard. I was told the story of the boy who killed a giant. Then there were the three guys who stood up for what was right and were thrown in the fire but didn't get burned. I marveled at the story of the guy who was thrown into a pit full of hungry lions but never got eaten. These were great stories, but that's all that they were, just stories. They remained as fairytales to me.

If this God was as strong as these stories made Him out to be then why couldn't He stop me from doing evil? Why couldn't He stop my father's substance abuse and drinking? Why wasn't He stopping the beatings my father showered on me regularly? Why was I the focus of his hate? Why couldn't God just save me then? Was I to believe the God that kept the fire from burning Shadrach, Meshach and Abednego, miraculously shut the mouths of those lions who wanted to eat Daniel and helped David overcome the giant–but couldn't rescue me from a beating just once? No, it was easier to think it was all fake than to think He really did those things. What had God ever given me? This was how I thought, and it's what kept me from really trusting God. It's what made me doubt everything I was hearing.

Peter was still the love of my life. He started coming to church with me on Sundays which was fun because we played in the van and even sang songs. Caring for him, however, became a lot harder for me because my father expected me to do everything after I got home from school. I entertained him, changed his diapers, fed him and bathed him. I did everything until my mother got home, and I was still expected to do my homework and clean up the kitchen. It wasn't too bad because having him gave me someone to play, talk and laugh with. Many times I would carry him into my room and stay there as long as I could. I read books to him and we would play pretend. This was a good distraction for me from my father's growing substance abuse and drinking.

I was ten years old in December of 1987 when my family took a trip back to Jamaica. It was seven years since I had seen James. I also saw some of my other family members of whom I had lost memory. It was a good time and I found things very interesting. As young as I was when we left, I remembered living there. James and I were not the same. I had almost forgotten him. The truth was I actually forgot why I wanted to be with him so much. We were different with each other now.

We spoke a little, but my personality and aggression was too much for him. I was more of an annoyance to him than anything. It hurt having to leave, but also because I had gone one week without being beaten. I knew going back to America meant everything would go back to the way it was.

When we returned to America, it was life as usual. My father was not different and neither was I. I returned to school to take my position as the bad girl. After Christmas break my teacher was replaced with another one. I don't know what it was, but something about this new lady made me dislike her. I wanted to rebel against her every request. If Miss. Brown said to take the gum out of my mouth, I chewed it louder. If she made me spit it out, I just put another piece in my mouth. I was her worse nightmare and I made her life as a teacher very rough. I became more defiant and didn't care what the consequences were. I knew my father was going to find out, but I did it anyway. I don't know why I didn't care (I had issues).

The threats from my dad would just increase the more he drank. One time he told me he couldn't stand me and that he was going to beat me until I couldn't wear skirts anymore because of the scars on my legs. He told me, "I'm going to whip you until I leave your back full with scars and you will be too embarrassed to show it." What a great goal to work towards. My father hated me and he was not hiding it anymore. He started telling me how he was going to kill me and that one day he would do it. He told me I was good for nothing and that he wanted to give me up.

Eventually my body started breaking down. I was constantly sick with stomach issues. I found myself at the doctor's a lot because of my reoccurring stomach pains. I know now it was because of the abuse and stress I was going through. I would have anxiety attacks while walking home. My heart would start beating out of my chest. I couldn't contain it at times and found myself in tears by the time my foot stepped on our sidewalk.

AS THE DAYS GO BY

A month or so after we returned from Jamaica I was in school at lunch. I was going to throw my food away when the boys at the table behind me thought it would be funny to lift my skirt up and expose my panties. Needless to say, I retaliated. Why wouldn't this go away? When was I going to get a break? Was this forever? I cannot explain to you how weary

I was of all this fighting. A teacher got me off the boy, separated me and placed me at a totally different table.

The next day, I was totally surprised when I was called out of class, taken into a room downstairs and saw my father. The teacher explained what I did. I assumed that since I was sticking up for myself, I had nothing to worry about. Then she proceeded to tell him everything I was doing and how I had been so disrespectful and aggressive. Before my teacher could finish speaking, my father started slapping me repeatedly in the face. Then he took off his belt and proceeded to whip me in the middle of the school office. Was this really happening? Here? I looked at the door and saw kids from the other classes starting to gather. I was so mortified by each blow. The fight or flight attitude came to me. He wasn't going to stop and the teacher sat behind her desk watching! He was going to kill me here, I thought. So I grabbed the belt and held on for dear life, I absolutely refused to let go. My father was shocked and demanded that I let go, but I refused. At that moment he started wrestling with me to pry the belt out of my hand. Now, my father was a small man, but he was very strong especially to a girl of ten. As angry as he was, he could not get it out of my hand. My mind was in survival mode because I knew that holding on to the belt meant I was going to get it worse once I let go.

When he saw he was not able to rip it out my hand, he got desperate and threw me on the floor. He started sitting on my chest to pry the belt out of my hands (What was happening here?!). When my grip did not budge, he got up and stepped on my head and face pulling to get the belt from my grip. As I write this, I am remembering the horror. His hatred, anger and pure resentment for me were clear. What father does this to his own child? What father would put their dirty boots in their child's face? When he finally yanked it out of my hand, he picked me up and prepared to continue beating me. But before he could strike me one more time, I dashed out of the office and ran down the hallway screaming at the top of my lungs for help. I screamed, "He's going to kill me! Help me, someone!"

I kept running. I didn't even know where I was going. I saw an exit door and that became my goal. When I looked behind me, my father was right there chasing after me. I was so close to the exit when my father grabbed me and yanked me back. I screamed and fought to get away as hard as I could. He covered my mouth and told me to shut up. As he dragged me back down the hallway, he was met by the principal and security officers. They took both of us into a room and sat us down.

Honestly, I cannot remember what happened. But they took us to different rooms and asked me a few questions. I sat in that office with urine all over me because through the whole ordeal I had lost control of my bladder. They ended up calling my mother who was mortified to hear about what had happened. She asked me to explain. I could tell she was so distraught. I was a wreck when I heard her voice. I gave her a summary of what just took place, but she could barely understand me since I was so hysterical.

I was left in the room while they spoke to my father. The school counselor asked me a few questions. I didn't answer truthfully because I knew he was in the next room. If he heard me say anything wrong I would just get into more trouble later. One of the questions the counselor asked was, "Do you like your father?" I thought, "Really lady? Did you not just hear what happened?" I hated his guts and I wanted to kill him myself if I could. I hated everything about him right then and there. If I was given a weapon, I would have used it and not thought twice. I wanted to bring great pain to him and make it slow. This was the thinking of a ten year old who had just beaten in school in front of her classmates. Hate for him was still too affectionate of an emotion. I loathed him and I lost any ounce of respect I had left for him that day. There was nothing he could do to get it back. I wanted nothing to do with him. If someone killed him in cold blood I would have taken the few pennies I had and given it to them for freeing me from this prison he had made for me.

In response to her question, however, I said, "Yes." How could I have said "no" thinking she would tell him my response. Then they asked me if I was okay going home with my father. I thought of the idea of going home with him and getting beat again or being forced to go back to my classroom in my soiled pants to be the laughing stock of my class. I took my chances with going home and literally being beaten to death.

I knew I was going to have to face my classmates, but I was not ready. I got in the car that day with my father who never said one word to me. He never even looked in my direction. He drove like I was not even in the car. When he got to the apartment, he didn't park, he just told me to get out. My father just dropped me off at the apartment and drove off.

It took a few weeks for things to die down at home and at school. I was humiliated beyond belief, I wanted to die. I wanted to kill myself or run away. I started thinking of how I could run away somewhere. Yet, I had nowhere to go. I felt God tell me to be still, there was a greater danger out there than my father if I went out into the world alone. What could possibly be worse than this? I could not find the courage to leave, so I abandoned the idea of running away. I know now that if I had left Satan would have had a ball with me. There was a greater danger out there and I knew it was more sensible to just stick it out here.

I could barely hold my head up high at school. I was now looked at as the girl who was beaten in school by her dad. Every grade knew about it because I ran down the hall screaming at the top of my lungs for help. I got the looks and the snickers, but I wasn't bullied. You would think I would have crawled under a rock and behaved myself. You would think I would have tried to walk the straight and narrow, but I was angry and ticked off. I hated every teacher in that school because they watched as I was beat. They didn't even open their mouths and tell him to stop. I didn't care if it was my own teacher or another teacher, I hated them. No one thought to call his name and snap him out of it. So I became the worst behaved kid in my fifth grade class. Even after the incident, I was going to show my anger. I felt there was nothing worse that could happen but my father beating me, literally to death. And at this point, I wanted it. I was openly defiant and begged for Miss. Brown to call my father. It was like I wanted everyone to see that fear would not control me.

I had something to prove and I wanted to show it. I will never forget the look on Miss Brown's face when she told me to spit out the gum I was so enthusiastically chewing a few weeks after the incident. I stuck out my tongue for her to see it and kept chewing. She said, "You better throw out that gum or else I will call your father." The whole class listened. In the past those words would have put me on the straight path, but not this time. They watched as I said, "Call him." I actually repeated my phone number to her and said, "Go ahead, do it. All he's going to do is beat me." I was so bold that if I was near the phone I would have dialed it myself. I cannot explain to you the look this teacher gave me when I said that. I said it with such a straight face not showing any fear while inside I was screaming to myself, "SHUT UP!!! What are you doing? Do you know what you are saying?"

For some reason Miss Brown was my target for the remainder of the year, maybe because I didn't like her and she was just a representative of all the teachers who watched me and didn't do anything. My behavior continued to be unacceptable, but I met with no repercussions from home. My parents no longer addressed my behavior at school. It was almost like I didn't exist anymore. There was this one day when my father told me to do something. I didn't do it the way he wanted. Normally he would have beaten the daylights out of me, but this day he just looked at me and said, "If I could, I would kill you. You're so lucky I can't touch you." What did that mean? Why couldn't he touch me?

I later found out when I was much older that Child Protective Services was called and my parents were under surveillance. They were told that if either one of them laid a hand on me for the next year CPS would step in. During that time my parents were trying to finish the process of getting their green cards so the last thing they wanted was anything that would cause a problem with immigration.

It is at this time I want to tell you that as bad as my situation was, God was by my side the whole time, even though I was not saved. In all of this, my parents never stopped me from going to church. There were times I went to church with black and blues and no one put two and two together. I lied to them and told them I got into a fight, which was true nine times out of ten. My parents never took church from me and never threatened it as a punishment. I was always allowed to go. That's how I knew that God never left me.

I am so afraid to think of where I would be now if I was not allowed to go to church. I honestly think I would have been dead. Parents, you have no idea the impact those two hours make once a week. You have no idea what your child may be facing. It is worth saying again? When we place our children in extracurricular activities that take them away from church on Sundays, we are just setting them up for failure. I plead with you to give your children the opportunity to thrive in a harsh world by being the example and putting God first. If my father who was unsaved and abusive never did it, how much more should we as saved believers do for our own children.

The story isn't over yet. It hasn't even started.

Chapter 6

THE GOD OF SECOND CHANCES

The year that my parents were under surveillance was a good period of time without any physical abuse. In fact, God used this time to start softening my heart. The fights in school slowly stopped because after the last incident, no one wanted to deal with my crazy dad. I also stopped being the bully, mostly because everyone pretty much stayed out of my way. There were those moments, but for the most part change had started in me. I still hadn't given my life over to God but I started considering everything taught at church because honestly nothing else was working. I needed love and I didn't feel it anywhere else.

WHO DO YOU SMELL LIKE?

God gave me a wonderful teacher my last year of elementary school–Ms. Williams. It was her first year in my school and when I saw her for the first time, she commanded respect. She brought such a different presence with her like no other teacher did from the years before. She made me want to make her proud of me. I wanted to do good and behave just for her. I looked up to her and I became a totally different student because of her. My grades improved drastically from the year before with Miss Brown, who ultimately left the school after half a year with me (Sorry Miss Brown wherever you are). What was it about this teacher that enabled her to get me to do what others weren't able to accomplish? I absolutely loved that woman.

I can't tell you that she talked with me one on one about life or that she encouraged me to live better. She was just very motivating. I soon grew to admire her like a mother figure. The kids in class started calling me teacher's pet. On many occasions I wanted to pound them into the ground, but because I was trying to please her I refrained as much as I could. There was one new kid who had been taunting me and who knew I didn't want to fight, but he kept egging me on. Finally, I waited till after school on our way home. We walked a good distance from the school and then I showed him what I was capable of. I didn't want anyone to twist the truth–I was going to defend myself if I needed to.

After graduating, I bumped into Ms. Williams outside of school and it was then she told me she was a Christian. It made so much sense and it made a world of difference having her in the school.

Just as it was with Brother and Sister Anderson, it was nothing that Ms. Williams said that started this change in me, it was what she gave off emotionally that made me feel everything was going to be okay with the world. That is the job of Christians, to give off an aroma of Christ.

"For we are to God the pleasing aroma of Christ among those who are being saved and those who are perishing. To the one we are an aroma that brings death; to the other, an aroma that brings life. And who is equal to such a task?" 2 Corinthians 2: 15-16 (NIV)

Friend, my short life was perishing fast and these believers gave the fragrance of life to me. I want to encourage you if you are trying to witness to unbelievers–bring the Word but bring the "Cologne of Jesus Christ" on you as well. Let them know you have been spending time with Jesus.

My pastor has very powerful cologne, which I personally love. There have been times when I have greeted him on a Sunday morning and then after the service is over, I could still smell the faint aroma of his cologne on my clothes, as did others who hugged me. One day, I was talking to someone outside church when my pastor called me on my phone. He asked if I was with that person. I told him yes, so he asked me to tell him to come to his office for a minute. I waited outside for the person to come back, and when he returned he had the pastor's cologne on him even though he hadn't hugged him.

It was just because he had been in the pastor's office that he carried the fragrance.

Let me tell you that's how it is supposed to be with Christ. We are to have the sweet smell of Christ on us, not the stench of this world. Believe it or not, if you are wallowing in sin and things that corrupt the soul, people will have a harder time believing you because you don't smell any different than them. When you've been with Christ, you immediately give off a scent that you are different. You must spend time with Jesus. Then, maybe, the lost will be more attracted to you.

MY FATHER ... WHO ART IN HEAVEN

My father did not lay a hand on me for over a year, but it didn't make me any less fearful of him. His anger was showing up more and more towards those outside the house. We lived on the fourth floor of a seven floor apartment building. On the fifth floor, directly above us, there was a boy by the name of Steven who was about two years older than me and who was nasty and rude. I also thought he was cute, but anyway. Our apartment door was one away from the elevator. One summer day Peter and I were waiting for the elevator so we could go outside to ride our bikes and play. When the elevator door opened Steven and his friends were there. We started getting on the elevator when he stood in front of the bike and pushed us out of the elevator. He told us to take the next one and started to snicker as the door closed.

What Steven didn't know is that my father was listening from inside our apartment door waiting for us to get on the elevator. He immediately came out of our apartment and asked why we didn't get on. We told him what happened and he lost it. My father took the stairs and rang Steven's bell. His mother answered the door and my father demanded that Steven come to the door. His mother was a sweet woman and kept asking my dad what happened. My father was so enraged that he ran back downstairs, went in his room and then went back upstairs. I didn't know exactly what was happening, but all we could hear was my father and Steven's mother yelling at each other from the fourth floor. I found out later that he had pulled a loaded gun on that thirteen year old boy. His mother had jumped in front of the gun and stood between my father and her son and told him if he was going to kill anyone, he should kill her. My father put the gun down and told both of them that if Steven ever came near Peter and me again he would shoot him where he stood. This was the kind of man with whom I was living—one who pulls a gun out on a thirteen year old just because he didn't let his kids take the elevator. This was my father. So when I tell you I took his threat of wanting to kill me seriously, you can understand why. He was a sick man and was only getting sicker.

Now the real story starts. After graduation from 6th grade, I spent the summer thinking about God more. In August of 1989, I was scheduled to enroll in one of the toughest middle schools in my area. I was sitting in my room when out of nowhere fear gripped me like it hadn't before. It was like a chill came down me as I heard God speak to me and say . . .

"It's time to give your heart to me. You will not survive what's coming without me."

I knew deep in my heart and soul He was right. I heard stories about this school and none were pleasant. I had already felt something serious was going to happen while in middle school and I feared I would not come out of it alive.

"Why won't you give your heart to me?" He asked as I began to cry.

"But I have tried before and I just couldn't do it. I'm too dirty and bad to serve you. I'm going to mess up and then I'll have to start all over again."

"Yes, you will mess up, but we will try again. I'll tell you now; I am not here to stop everything. I'm here to comfort you and give you strength in those scary moments. I will lead you, guide you and change you."

I had never felt such a pulling in all my life. We had spoken before, but this was different. Much later in life I came across a verse that reminded me of this exact moment I had with God.

John 6:44

"No one can come to Me unless the Father who sent Me draws them and I will raise them up at the last day. It is written in the Prophets: 'They will all be

taught by God. Everyone who has heard the Father and learned from Him comes to Me.'" (NIV)

I was being drawn at that very moment, and I could not resist it one bit. I got down on my knees next to my bed, and with tears that could not be stopped, I finally gave my life over to Jesus Christ. All the doubt and skepticism left me. I felt like a waterfall had welled up in me. It started washing all the dirt away that made me feel I was unworthy. I will never be able to fully explain the feeling I had at that very moment. I could do nothing but cry hysterically as the power of God was felt for the first time.

I don't know where you are in your walk with the Lord, but let me tell you Jesus loves you. I know I said it before and you have probably heard it said by others, but know this, <u>God's love is not to be compared to man's</u>. Man's love and dedication is conditional no matter how much they may say otherwise. We love people when they reward us with love in return or show us strong appreciation. We love out of passion and emotion. Jesus' love, however, is not driven by emotion or passion and does not decrease because of our imperfection or even our hate towards Him. He does not love you because you love Him back. His love is not because you do everything right or because you're a good person. His love is for all no matter who it is. It is a love that is unwavering and there is nothing on earth to which you can compare it.

Jesus didn't die on the cross for you because He felt like it. He also didn't do it to be accepted by all. He did it because He embodies the true meaning of Love. It is patient, gentle, not boastful, unwavering and perfect. It is not dependent on your response or on how much you sin or do good works. It is what it is because He is God.

Jeremiah 31:3 was a verse I came across years later in my walk with God.

"The Lord hath appeared of old to me saying, 'Yea, I have loved thee with an everlasting love: therefore with loving-kindness have I drawn thee'". (KJV)

God did not draw me with guilt, fear, or condemnation. Instead, He drew me with unfailing loving-kindness. It makes so much sense! This was why I was drawn to the Andersons and Miss Williams. They showed unfailing kindness to me and God used them to break down the walls I built to fortify my heart. That "kindness" was the door God used to enter into my life.

Jesus may have physically died 2000 years ago, but He still meets us today right where we are. I was deep in sin and in a pit no one could get me out of. My thoughts were desperately wicked at eleven years of age, and there was no amount of counseling that could remove that. I needed my God because without Him nothing was going to get better—and it is the same for everyone. If you are battling addictions, rage, lust, or un-forgiveness, know that He can show you a love that is able to pull you out of your pit. I say this to you with all certainty, simply because I am living proof of His forgiveness.

For those reading who may be leaders or who are trying to lead someone to Christ, show kindness. Conviction will take place, but it's kindness, love, patience and a firm hope that will draw a person. And you know what, you may not be the one to see it happen. I never saw the Andersons again, so they have no idea what happened to me. They have no idea where I am and what they did for me. They put four years into me and then someone else took over. Don't give up on a person because you don't get to eat the fruit of your labor right away. There may be some sacrifices that will only yield a heavenly reward, and isn't that the important part?

I DO WHAT I HATE TO DO

"I don't understand what I do. I don't do what I want to do. Instead, I do what I hate to do. I do what I don't want to do." Romans 7:15-16a (NIV)

Paul got it right; God did not erase my past or remove the abuse in my home immediately. For His own reasons, He chose not to. I know now there was still a lot of work to be done. I tried to avoid altercations with people as best as

I could, but it wasn't working. I continued finding myself having to deal with my rage more and more.

I knew it was really bad when one day at church, a boy kept taunting me. I ignored him several times before but this day I was just fed up. As he was mouthing off to me, I swung at him and the monster was loose. My friend Sally was there. She tried to stop me, but I was so full of rage I began fighting both her and the boy. The leaders finally got me off of the boy, but Sally had bruises all over her arm from the blows I threw. I needed to learn self control and fast. Most of my fights were with boys. I won a majority of them, but the feeling of victory was swallowed up by guilt and shame now.

It became normal for me to come home with a black eye. My mother told me at one point she was so afraid I was going to lose my eye because of all the fights I would get into. My mother witnessed the rage in me one day when a girl had pushed me too far. My mother tried to stop me, but she couldn't get a good grip on me. It took two more adults to help my mom separate me from this girl. She could not believe my rage, and she could not control it. Only one person could, and I needed Him to do it fast.

This new walk with God was a seriously slow process. I would be so angry with myself because I was unable to be who I knew God wanted me to be. And at the same time, I battled tremendously with my sexual addiction. God's love helped me deal with all these issues, but it wasn't in my time, it was in His. He told me this was not the life He had for me.

He wanted me to trust Him more. My rage and addiction were just results of my inability to trust God.

I needed to change and He wanted to help me change. You may already know this, but allow me to say it anyway. In order for God to change someone, He doesn't wave a magic wand over you that will transform you by its touch. We are who God made us and He isn't going to get rid of that, but He does remove all the imperfections that attach themselves to us in life and through sin. There were things I was still responsible for and things I still needed to learn. He needed me to learn this Scripture:

Jeremiah 18:1-4
"This is the word that came to Jeremiah from the LORD: 'Go down to the potter's house, and there I will give you my message.' So I went down to the potter's house, and I saw him working at the wheel. But the pot he was shaping from the clay was marred in his hands; so the potter formed it into another pot, shaping it as seemed best to him." (NIV)

It's like God had it in his mind that I would be a vase, but I became marred and damaged. He never changed his plans for me to be a vase, it was just that now God needed to form me over again and shaped me as He saw fit. That's what He does to all of us. God knows what He wants us to be, but when the blows of life come up against us we become damaged and bruised. God doesn't throw us out or put us on a shelf to rot. He picks us up and starts all over again. I am reminded of the times when I would play with Play-Dough. At times hair and maybe a little pebble or dirt would get into it. I had to inspect the dough and remove all those things that made it lumpy. Then after I went through it I started to roll it out and form it. In the same way, God cannot make you into that beautiful vessel without taking the time to remove those things in your life that are not pleasing and lumpy.

God doesn't just shape us, He also cleans us up so that we can be a perfect masterpiece. Our God is a perfectionist and doesn't do anything half heartedly. Good art takes inspiration and time. There is no way you can clean yourself up enough to deserve God. If we could clean ourselves up, then why did Jesus die on the cross for our sins? He came to do for us what we could not naturally do for ourselves. When I was a child going to Sunday School and Children's Church, they always talked about how Jesus' blood washed us and we became whiter than snow. He took the blackness in our hearts and made it white like the wool of sheep. It always confused me how red blood was supposed to make everything white, but as I continued with the Lord I totally understood the process.

After we accept Christ, God doesn't push a button that wipes away our desire to sin (Although that would be cool). When I gave my life over to the Lord, I still had desires that didn't match up with my new life. I know I am not alone in this experience. There are very few people I have met who have struggled deeply before coming to the Lord, but then–after salvation–saw the desire to continue in those struggles end. For most people, we must continue to walk that road a bit longer. Slowly dying to the flesh as Paul puts it.

A famous teacher has told the story several times of how her and her husband were both heavy smokers before they were saved. When they received salvation, the Lord dealt with her husband and he stopped smoking immediately. She, on the other hand, worked hard to get rid of that desire. I was in the same boat as this teacher. I was saved and God was dealing with me about some things I could not easily break. God was not going to leave me alone in my mess though. He walked along this road with me and showed me love when I was victorious and also when I was not so victorious. I realized I was beaten down and needed to allow God to do the fixing in my life, not me or anyone else, only God.

Chapter 7

WHEN MY LIFE CHANGED FOREVER

"For our light and momentary troubles are achieving for us an eternal glory that far outweighs them all. So we fix our eyes not on what is seen, but on what is unseen, since what is seen is temporary, but what is unseen is eternal." 2 Corinthians 4:17-18 (NIV)

I came across this scripture one day and held strongly to its words as things began escalating in my life. I felt God wanted me to know that the things I had seen and the things I was going to see were just temporary. What I did not see would be eternal. What I saw was my father's hate, my mother's absence, my own hurt and pain, as well as my anger and my aggression. If the scripture was true, then this all would be temporary. In my natural mind, I found such a statement hard to comprehend. It was hard to imagine a life without all the chaos and turmoil around me. How could I? This was the life I had known for so long. No matter how I behaved or where I went, there was always some sort of pain to follow.

The "Unseen," well, that was my life with God. It was my future, my victory over this life that was "Seen." The idea that one day my dad would no longer beat me and that I would have Jesus as well as a family to love me was too far from me. I truly cannot explain to you how important this verse was to me. It was my only hope. It was the thing that kept me from giving up on everything. I had chosen to hold on to the invisible and the unseen and believe that one day I would let go of what was seen. That was a tough thing to do, but every day I loosened my grip.

THE TOUGH GOT TOUGHER

Now that I was serving the Lord I tried to do things differently. I started praying for myself and praying for my parents. I asked God to help me do the right thing and not be defiant. My younger brother was now about 4 years old. He was not talking, so my parents thought something might be wrong with him. But he and I spoke all the time. Peter , for some reason, did not talk to my parents. Whenever my father asked him a question, Peter froze up. Depending on the situation, he would get whipped as well. He didn't get it as bad as I did, but when he did get hit, it was over the top.

After school, I was in charge of picking up Peter from daycare and bringing him home. One day I was off from school and my father told me to meet him at 4:00.p.m. at the bus stop so he could take me to the daycare to pick up my brother. It was about 5 or 6 blocks away from my building. I started getting ready, but I got engrossed in a TV show I was watching. To this day I don't know what happened, but I totally lost track of time and when I looked it was 4:10. By now you can imagine the fear I had when I saw the time. I grabbed everything I had and ran to the corner, but by the time I got to the corner my father was driving home. He saw me, but he didn't stop to pick me up. I knew what was awaiting me. By this time the CPS case had been withdrawn. So my father was going to let loose on me, something he had not been able to do in months.

Any other parent would have asked what happened, but I wasn't dealing with any other parent. I turned around and slowly started walking back home. With every step I thought of running away and not returning. I thought of different ways of getting out of this, but there was nothing I could do. I began to pray. I asked God to keep him from whipping me. I prayed as hard as I could, and I planned that if he did hit me, I would not shed a tear. Those days were over. I was stronger now, and I had Jesus on my side. I refused to let him take the joy God had given me.

When I got home, my father asked me what happened. I told him I lost track of the time. He told me to go into my room. A minute later he met me with his leather belt. He started whipping me, but I refused to cry. I don't know what was hurting more, the blows, or the painful words he was saying to me and the names he was calling me. I would not give him that satisfaction of seeing a single tear fall. My last beating was in school. He was used to make me break down, but this time I took it, no crying. He started hitting me as if he wanted to make up for all the months of wanting to but couldn't. I just stood there and took every blow. Eventually, I was getting hit so much that I fell on the bed. Peter couldn't take it anymore and started screaming. Before I knew it, my Peter ran in front of my father and jumped on me. He took a few blows for me. My father was in such a rage that he didn't even realize he had been hitting Peter.

He stopped and told my brother to go, but Peter wouldn't leave me. He picked Peter up and put him to the side. He then proceeded to hit me more, and he eventually abandoned the belt and started slapping me in my face repeatedly. I think the reason he wouldn't stop was because I showed no emotion. When my father finished, he stepped back and said, "I am going to kill you one day. You play with your mother, but you won't play with me. I will kill you." I sat there as Peter ran to me once my father left the room. That is when I finally cried. He held me, and I cried in my little brother's arms.

After a few minutes, I walked to the bathroom to clean myself up. As I was walking, I realized my underwear was soiled. He had hit me that hard. My father somehow realized it as well and told me to pull my underwear down. When he saw I had soiled myself he laughed at me. Pleased with what he had accomplished, he looked me right in the face and said, "See I told you, I'm in control. I made you crap on yourself. I am going to whip you so bad that your legs and back are striped. You won't be able to wear a skirt ever again." Then he walked away laughing at me. He continued taunting me as he walked by the bathroom. I felt like trash at that moment. I had thought he could not humiliate me anymore than he had already done. I was wrong. That day he was able to bring me lower than I had ever felt before. It was like fighting in school all over again, except this time my father was the bully.

That night when my mom came home, my father was out. I was getting ready for my shower. My mom must have noticed the swelling on my face. She asked me to lift up my shirt. She saw the markings on my back; they were thick welts that hurt just by blowing on them. She inspected my wounds, like she had many times before and then stepped back. It was quiet for a few seconds, then she said, "You probably deserved it." What? Are you kidding me? I deserved to be slapped in my face repeatedly and beaten till I soiled my pants just because I lost track of the time and was late? If that beating didn't shatter my self-esteem, her one sentence did.

I have always felt one of the biggest lies told to children is the saying, "Sticks and stones may break my bones, but words will never hurt me." Telling a child to ignore being called names because it does not matter . . . that is just not true. Words do hurt, especially if the words come from those who are supposed to uplift and protect you. It's not just my view either; the Bible says the same thing.

"The soothing tongue is a tree of life, but a perverse tongue crushes the spirit." Proverbs 15:4 (NIV)

My spirit was crushed by the thought that all the pain and abuse I had experienced was something I "deserved." Those simple words from my mother hurt me emotionally and mentally as much as my father's beating did physically.

My mind froze when I heard her say that. It then began to flood with other thoughts. "She has no idea how he treats me! He doesn't treat me like his daughter, but like a stranger he fights with in the street. I'm trying to be good, I am!"

I got into the shower and cried. I was trying to be good, and yet I still couldn't meet their standards. My conclusion was that I was a mistake. I was more of a burden to them than anything. My mother was once everything to me–my only source of love. And now the place she held in my heart was ripped out of me like a page in a notebook and crumbled up. She had no idea that I would have given my life for her because she was MY pride and joy. From that point on I looked at her in a different way.

THE MOMENT THAT DEFINED MY FUTURE

Later that day, when it was time for dinner, we all came together at the table. My father looked at my face and said,

"When you go to school and they ask you what happened to your face tell them I beat you because you're a good for nothing wretch." My mother interjected and said, "No, she is not going to say that." I hated him. I hated the air he breathed. When he said that my heart began beating hard inside my chest. It felt just like those times before I would get ready to fight. I wanted to shove my fork in his throat and laugh while he suffered.

When he put his head down to eat, I looked at him thinking to myself, "I have to kill you. I'm going to kill YOU tonight." When we finished dinner, I went into my room and got ready for bed. I replayed everything in my head. It filled me with anger. I made up my mind that tonight I would kill him in his sleep. My plan was to wake up in the middle of the night, take a knife from the kitchen and stab him in his sleep. "I can do this," I thought to myself. I knew my father was a medium sleeper and that I could easily hover over him long enough to do it.

This was my state of mind. I was tired of being a victim and wanted to be free. I wanted peace and I had a plan that would, supposedly, give it to me. That night I woke up at 1 or 2 in the morning and went to the kitchen. I was really going to attempt this. But thank you Jesus–that voice returned.

"You need to trust me."

"But look at what he's doing to me. Did you hear what he said to me? I hate everything about him and I want to kill him right where he sleeps," I said.

He just repeated himself, "You must trust me."

At that moment, a humongous peace came over me and the anger that was boiling inside of me was removed. That irritated me because I had nothing to fuel me. I returned to bed, placed my head on the pillow, and in one breath I fell asleep. Most people would think I dreamt the whole thing. It sounds like it was a dream. It wasn't. It happened, and I thank God I listened.

WALKING IN HIS WORD

I served the Lord as best as I could, but my home life made it very hard. I started getting anxious every time I heard my father's keys jingling on the doorknob. Part of my home responsibilities included having the kitchen completely clean and the cushions of the couch placed to my father's specifications. In the past, I received a few smacks to the face and on the head for not placing the cushions properly on the couch. No matter how hard I tried, my dad would always find something wrong with the kitchen.

I had God. Don't ask me how exactly, but even though I was eleven years old, my faith in Him gave me the strength to go on. I started to pray more, and as I did, my desire for God increased. The situations were still present, but my perspective of them had changed. Again, don't ask me how. I simply believed. What I could not shake off though was this feeling I had within me that something was still missing. That something was my mother. Yes, she hurt me, but I wanted to love her the way I used to.

She found a better job in the medical field, and I was very proud of her. She had made the decision to go back to school and received her degree. The problem was that now she spent more time at work and she was never able to be with me. My resentment towards her grew more and more. She would walk in from working hard and she wouldn't have the strength to even talk with me for 10 minutes. My father made it clear he didn't want me around her. The moment my mom would come home he made me go into my room so she could have peace and quiet.

I started to tell her I wanted to be with her more–and even if her excuses were valid I took them all as rejection. Why couldn't she take me out for one hour and talk to me about the changes in my body? I was changing and I needed her help. She never gave me "The Talk." I remember asking desperately if she could just spend time with me. When I was younger I at least got a book at bedtime. I wanted answers for the things I was feeling in my body. I wanted her to explain to me love and relationships, but she had neither the time nor the patience.

My little brother, Peter , was truly my only companion. I look at it now and see how God used him to help sustain me through the trials of my life. We would make games out of anything. On many occasions, we would walk to the post office, which was quite a distance away from home. If we came across a bottle in the street, we would see how far we could kick it before it broke. Sometimes we would race from one end of a block to the other. It made our travels much more fun. God used my little brother in the simplest ways during my childhood. Even though I lived in a world of chaos, I was still able to experience some true joy.

Thank you Lord for blessing me with my little brother.

As my love for God grew, I still felt this sense of hopelessness. I would think to myself often, "Will this ever get better?" I really struggled with the idea that this was the life I was meant to live forever. I cried just about every single day. As I walked home from school my throat would get a lump in it and tears would stream down my face. I did not want to go home. I tried to fight it as much as I could. I tried to convince myself it would all be okay, but it was too overwhelming.

Before, I would use fighting to help me control my emotions. It was what helped me express myself and relieve the fear and anger kept inside. However, I didn't want to be what I once was anymore. My new life with Christ called me to be someone new, but I hated my current life of abuse with every passing breath. It was getting to the point where I was thinking of ways to get out. I revisited maybe running away or even suicide. There were so many times I remember praying desperately to get cancer or something like it. I heard of young kids my age getting deadly diseases, and I thought they were lucky if they got to die. I just wanted anything that would take my life and take me away from all I knew.

I was not allowed to cry in front of my father, just like when I was younger. If he knew I was crying, he would hit me even more. His logic was, "If you cry for no reason, I will provide you with a really good reason to cry." I had so many emotions running through me, but I wasn't allowed to express them in his presence. There were times when I used to go into the bathroom to take a shower and I would lock the door, sit on the toilet and cry silently.

At times, I would put a little soap in my eyes so that if anyone noticed my red eyes I would have an answer. There were times when I felt like screaming so hard, but instead I would just hold myself as tight as I could, rock back and forth with my mouth open and scream without a sound coming from my mouth.

It was only at night when everyone was asleep I would feel some peace and a sense of safety. Those were my special moments with God. He would come and meet with me in my world. I would talk with Him about everything. I would talk to him about my day and about my pains. I'd ask Him about things that confused me. Sometimes I'd receive answers, other times my questions were answered with other questions. Then there were the times when I wouldn't get an answer to my question, instead He would say something like, "You will understand better in the future."

For some of you reading this, I know this may seem strange to you. "She talked with God? And He spoke back to her?" Yeah . . . that's what happened. He was there to listen and comfort me when I needed it. He was what kept me going. To be honest, I don't know how kids today who don't have Jesus in their lives make it in this world. What I do know, is that I would not be here today had God not made his presence known to me.

It would be many years later, during a very delicate time of my life, when I would see these verses–that for me–described what I went through:

> *"For troubles without number surround me;*
> *my sins have overtaken me, and I cannot see.*
> *They are more than the hairs of my head,*
> *and my heart fails within me.*
> *Be pleased, O Lord to save me;*
> *O Lord, come quickly to help me. May all who seek to*
> *take my life be put to shame and confusion;*
> *may all who desire my ruin*
> *be turned back in disgrace.*
> *May those who say to me, 'Aha! Aha!'*
> *be appalled at their own shame.*
> *But may all who seek you*
> *rejoice and be glad in you;*
> *may those who love your salvation always say,*
> *'The LORD be exalted!' Yet I am poor and needy;*
> *may the Lord think of me.*
> *You are my help and my deliverer;*
> *O my God, do not delay." Psalms 40: 12 -17 (NIV)*

I felt as if these verses were written just for me. God had seen everything that was happening and my deliverance was coming soon.

Read these verses:

> *"Rescue me from the mire,*
> *do not let me sink;*
> *deliver me from those who hate me,*
> *from the deep waters.*
> *Do not let the floodwaters engulf me*
> *or the depths swallow me up*
> *or the pit close its mouth over me. Answer me,*
> *LORD, out of the goodness of your love;*
> *in your great mercy turn to me.*
> *Do not hide your face from your servant;*
> *answer me quickly, for I am in trouble.*
> *Come near and rescue me;*
> *redeem me because of my foes."*
> *Psalms 69:14-20 (NIV)*

Have you ever felt desperate? Are you there now? Please hear me when I say God knows all your hurts and pains. These Psalms were written by David who had been through so much. Some of his pain was of his own doing, and some were from the attacks of his enemy. God could have allowed the Scriptures to only record the moments when David was victorious. He could have only allowed David's times of thanksgiving for victory over his enemies. Instead, God showed us David's times of weakness and vulnerability because He knew these very words would comfort someone like you and someone like me. You see, even though he grieved, David knew through it all his help came from the Lord. Do not be ashamed of the pains and struggles you face as you walk this walk. Cry out to Jesus. He is there for you.

It wasn't always easy for me to see God's hand in my situations. I remember one night in particular where I didn't feel His comfort at all. I had gotten into trouble for something stupid. To be honest, I don't even remember what I did, but I know it was stupid. I only remember that I was trying to explain to my parents what had happened. While doing so, I was told to shut up. Then all the vulgar comments were hurled at me by both of them. The things said to me by my mother broke my heart the most.

My mother wasn't perfect and I knew that. Whenever she would lose it with me, unlike my father, it was because I deserved it. With her the punishment would always fit the crime. This time however, I did nothing that deserved what was being thrown at me. Had it been only her yelling at me, I know this would have been different. Instead, she was joining in with my father at his level of insults in tearing me down. The whole thing left me hurt and wounded inside.

I went to my room, fell on my bed and cried in my pillow. Like every night, my God, my Friend, my Companion and

Comforter came to me to do what He did best, comfort me. But I didn't want to talk to Him.

"I don't want to hear from you right now. Nothing I do seems right. I try to listen to you and it's not working. They still hate me. Listen to them. Listen to what they are saying to me. I will never be good enough for them."

I actually heard God start to say something, but I cut Him off and said, "I don't want to hear it from you."

I knew what He was going to say to me. That He loved me and that I was good enough for Him, that He saw the truth and that's what mattered. But what mattered to me at that moment was letting Him know the "truth" was not changing my world at all. It was not doing anything for me.

My father came to the door; apparently He had not finished with all his accusations towards me. It was like throwing acid on an open wound. This time my mother stayed silent. Between his words and her silence, allowing him to say and call me such things, I felt so lost. To be honest, my mother's silence was all I heard. His words didn't hurt half as much as her silence.

That night, I cried . . . "God, why do you keep letting them do this to me? I can't take this anymore! You're just watching them do this. How much longer will this keep going before you do something? You have the power to stop all this, but you don't. You're just as bad as them! Please, just go away. I don't want to talk to you right now."

I just couldn't understand how God, with all His infinite power to stop all this, refused to do so. I was too hurt and I didn't want to be comforted by Him that night. You know what's strange? I felt God back off. I know now the Lord never leaves us, and I know He didn't that night. But He pulled back just enough to give me some space, and I know why. It was the weirdest feeling.

For almost two years, I would end my days running into His arms, feeling His love as if it were medicine for all my hurts. That was the first night in a long time I felt empty. It was also the very last time I ever said to God, "Go away!" because it was clear to me what a night spent out of His arms felt like. His love for me and the comfort He gave me each night was what made me feel peace strong enough to help me sleep and strength powerful enough to make me rise the next day. That night, neither of those things happened.

It was a short time after that when God brought me to the scripture from the beginning of this chapter, 2 Corinthians 4:17-18. I read it and heard him say to me, "I promise you this is all temporary. I am eternal, so keep your eyes on me. One day all of these things will be gone. Hold on and trust me." A day when I would be free from all this abuse, sorrow, pain and hurt? How was that going to happen? I had no idea, but I had decided I was going to try my best to make GOD happy.

BEING SET FREE

The first thing I got rid of was all the porn. I never looked at it again. I also made sure I wasn't friends with anyone who would encourage that temptation, instead I sought friendships with those who helped point me to God. These few changes helped me stop my addiction much more quickly.

The first day I chose not to give into my flesh, I felt God telling me I had the strength to resist.

> *"No temptation has seized you except what is common to man. And God is faithful; He will not let you be tempted beyond what you can bear. But when you are tempted, He will also provide a way out so that you can stand up under it."* **1 Corinthians 10:13 (NIV)**

Many times God provided me with a way out, but I chose not to take it. I loved my desires more than I loved God. This day, I would love my God more than my desire. I knew that with God's help I could do this, and so I did. It was my very first day of victory. Yes, I had moments when I wasn't as victorious, but I took control over my life that day. And eventually, broke free of my sexual struggle. Each day I fought to resist until it no longer had a hold on me.

One of the worst feelings in the world is when you are not in control of your own actions. Satan lures us into addictions by making us think we can control the sin without realizing it is the sin that begins to control us. We think we can start and stop whenever we want, but the more we give into our flesh, the more addictive it becomes. The sin, in a way, takes on a life of its own demanding to be satisfied.

This is why scripture tells us . . .

"Those controlled by sinful nature (the flesh) cannot please God." Romans 8:8 (NIV)

It is why we have to kill the flesh. This flesh lives, breathes and has a mind of its own. Do not underestimate the power of sin and addiction. It can become way too powerful, and before you know it, you're bowing down to do its bidding.

I have had the privilege of ministering to many people who struggled with different addictions, including sexual sin. The sad truth is, when they are ready to let go of their sin, their sin is not ready to let go of them. This sin does not let go so easily. So when I say I was set free, I know I am one of the few who were able to do so alone, without the help of others. I had no one to lean on but God. If you are finding that letting go of something like this is proving to be more than you can handle, find someone who will be an accountability partner. This is someone you trust and someone you know who will keep your secret and pray with you through this. I know it may be embarrassing, but we have to put aside our pride and allow our brother or sister in the Lord to help "carry your burdens" (**Galatians 6:2**), in order to truly be set free at times.

I did not have victory over this issue immediately. I had some days of victory and some days of defeat. Sometimes I was convinced that all my victories were erased when I messed up, but that was far from the truth. I had to learn to celebrate the victories and erase those days of defeat. I had to shake them off and continue forward. God saw I was not pleased with where I was and I was not giving up until my struggles were gone. I could not control everything in my life, but I was determined to control this.

Part Two

THE NEW ROAD I BEGAN

Chapter 8

A NEW ME

HE FINALLY CAME

Shortly after I decided to live my life for the Lord, the day I had long dreamt of arrived. James, my older brother, was finally joining us. Ten years of waiting was finally coming to a close. Mom told me that James received his visa and would be joining us within a month. My excitement was unexplainable. I later found out James was also a Christian. Now I was even more excited to have someone to talk to about Jesus. This was truly going to be a life changing moment for me. In all this, I can testify to the saying that "God is never late and he is never early, he is always on time." He could not have brought James to us, or should I say to me, at a better time.

The day he came home it was like fireworks had gone off in our home. It had been ten years of separation and now every one of us felt, that finally, our family was complete.

James was a handsome 18-year old young man who was both well-spoken and well-mannered. I could tell when I saw him that he had his own stories to tell, but a form of trust needed to be developed first before either of us would share our experiences. Hours passed as my parents spent time talking to him and looking at the different goodies he had brought. Before we knew it, it was time to head to bed.

Peter and I shared one room, and now James was going to join us. My parents were not able to afford a three bedroom apartment, so the three of us had to share. We didn't care. We were together. When bed time came, it was just us three and it was our time.

When I went to Jamaica at ten, I was not saved. I was so different this day compared to back then. When I was in Jamaica we did not bond very well. Looking back at it now, I know the reason we didn't bond was because of pain and hurt on his part. I was the one my parents picked to live with them in America. I would have been hurt too if there were two of us and I was left behind. He had every right to be hurt. I see that now. How could he bond with us when it looked like we moved on without him? I'm sure Peter looked like a replacement. There were many wounds that needed to be mended and it had to start somewhere.

That first night, James and I spoke for the first time alone. It was the absolute best. My parents bought a twin bed for James, while Peter and I shared a bunk bed. James would lie in his bed as we laughed and made jokes late into the night.

His laugh was so loud and powerful, it brought such a huge change to the house. I don't remember ever laughing so hard, or loud, before that time. He had a ton of questions for me about living in America, and I asked him about Jamaica. He helped me remember what it was like living in Jamaica, even though I only lived there for a short period of time.

SEEING IT DEEPER

James told me how he stayed in the homes of different family members, but that his time with our Aunt Val was the best of all. Then he talked to me about his own experiences with God. He asked me about my church and wanted to know what it was like. He was so excited because he could tell I was still a "Baby Christian" and there was much I still needed to learn. He wanted to teach me as best as he could about God. He wanted to introduce me to some new worship songs and other forms of Christian music. This was the beginning of not just a new life for me, but the beginning of a whole new world.

God used James in the best way. I had never met anyone like him in my whole life. I completely loved my church; it was a place where I found refuge. But in all the years of going to church, there was no one I had come across with the knowledge James had of the Word and of spirituality. He was knowledgeable in so many areas of Scripture and biblical history. I grew to love him and trust him.

I saw he was different. One day, while I was in bed, I struggled with reading a few verses in my Bible for devotion. Out of nowhere, James said to me from his bed, "The Lord told me you are not where you need to be with Him. He wants more from you. You're not reading enough. You must feed your spirit with more." I couldn't believe what I was hearing, God spoke to someone else?

See, my problem was I wanted to know more about God, but I didn't like reading much. Even though I spoke to God every night, it didn't increase my knowledge of Him. That is what His Word is for. It is there to provide us with the knowledge of who God is. God's Word is truth, and in His truth is the knowledge of who He is. To whoever is reading this, if you struggle in discovering the Lord for yourself, engross yourself in His Word. Learn how to see yourself in its pages, discover what God created us to be and learn about His love and mercy for all. Then, as you read and learn, live as the Scriptures instruct. When you do this, you will see God's Words come to life in you.

I wanted to know more, so I asked, "How do I give Him more?"

"I will teach you. I have a lot to teach you."

That is exactly what he did. I cannot explain the fire he helped light in me as I learned about a new side of God I never knew existed. I knew the Bible stories, but I never connected those stories to my own life. All the things I learned were surface things like, "God helped Moses because Moses trusted in Him. So, trust God when you need help." But, now I was able to connect. I saw that Moses had to wait on God, and that there were times when Moses was scared and felt tired and unequipped. I saw Moses had to go through some things in order to develop the relationship he had with God.

As James taught me about God, he also shared some of his own stories with me. There were many things he went through while he was in Jamaica. It isn't my place to mention them here, but one thing we did have in common was my dad and his abuse. His worst memory of my dad was when he was whipped at 6 years old.

James would go with my father to work at times. My dad would always send James to the store around the corner to get a newspaper for him. He would tell him to go straight to the store and come right back. One day, on the way to the store my brother saw a small pool of water that caught his attention, so he bent down to look in it. The pool of water had little tadpoles in it and James stopped to look at them. A few minutes had gone by and he rushed to the store, got the paper and ran back to my father.

When my brother brought the newspaper to my father he asked James, "Did you go straight to the store like I told you?"

"Yes," he said in fear.

He grabbed my brother and asked him again, but this time he took his belt off. Before James could speak, my father started beating him in the middle of the street. Now, in Jamaica, at least back then (maybe still today), it was not uncommon to beat your children, even in public. My father stopped hitting him, feeling satisfied by his discipline. But when those around saw him beating James, they actually egged him, on so he continued. For me, it explained why my father didn't think twice about beating me in the street and in school those times, because it was normal to him.

James eventually collapsed on the ground and was unable to stand. No matter how much my father threatened him, my brother wasn't physically capable of getting up. My father had to carry him home that day. My brother was not too sure of the events that followed, except that he knew my mother was angry and it caused major trouble between my parents. He had welts all over his body and it took days for him to recover. Again, for me, this story explained why my father would never beat me with my mother in the house. It also explained why my mother would always inspect my wounds when she heard he had whipped me.

James continued to provide several pieces to the puzzle. As we spoke about our father and his abuse, James told me that my father was abused worse than we ever were. On his back were scars of countless beatings he had as a child. My father had cuts and scars in his head because my grandmother took things like pots and wires and would beat him in the head with them. My father was the victim at one point of his own parents' rage. He was only able to give what he was taught.

A preacher shared a story in one of her messages of a female dog a family had. This dog was injured in some way and had lost the use of her back legs. At some point, she got pregnant and had pups. As these pups started to grow, the owner noticed the pups were only walking on their front paws. So the owner took all the pups to the vet. The vet saw nothing wrong with the pups' back legs. It was concluded they were walking that way because their mother couldn't teach them how to properly walk on all four legs because she herself couldn't.

Friend, do you know how that story hits home for me in so many ways? I have to tell you, as I got older, I understood more and more that my father was injured and that he could not use his "back legs." He could only use his front legs. He was a wounded soul and a product of his own upbringing. He never beat me in the head with a pot, but he did leave scars on my back and a pain in my heart. My father only knew hate, so that's what he gave back. I am not providing him an excuse and I'm not giving you an excuse either. The truth still remains, he needed Jesus.

Are you only using your front legs? Are there events in your life that have left you broken, wounded and lame? So much so, that those under you are restricted to only learn the same? Well, I want to encourage you to allow God to do a healing in you. Allow Him to stop this vicious cycle within you. Don't allow yourself to go one more day in a broken state. There are those counting on you to be whole. There are those looking to you to be that example. You need to spend time with God so he can heal the scars from your past and help you properly move forward.

I listened in amazement to my brother as he explained the different events my parents had gone through. When it was all over, even though many of my questions had been answered, I still had no sympathy for my father. In my mind, he was a villain and I was his victim. There was a lot that needed to be done in me before I would ever have sympathy for him.

LEARNING ABOUT THE ENEMY

My brother armed me with knowledge, but the best pieces of information he presented to me were those about being a soldier. My church rarely spoke of the enemy, the devil or demons. James came from a church that spoke a lot about the subject.

James helped me learn about our enemy. Knowledge of the Word alone does nothing for a believer. There is a greater requirement which is to live the Word. Satan and all his little minions fear the Christian who not only hears the Word, but who also applies it to his life by doing what it says. He is not afraid of you because you go to church. Luke 4:33 speaks about Jesus driving a demon from a man IN the synagogue. It isn't the written scripture alone that drives the forces of the enemy back. He knows the written Word, Satan quoted it to Jesus and tried to manipulate it to confuse and challenge Christ. Even prayer and fasting, if not done with humility and conviction will hold no weight against the enemy. The religious leaders prayed and fasted and yet they could not see the power within Christ. In fact, they attributed His power to the devil.

Before I go on, I want to make something clear–I believe many, not all, but many–Christians tend to give the devil more attention and credit than necessary. I have often heard Christians blame Satan for every single bad thing in their lives when in fact some of those tragedies they faced stemmed from bad choices they made. In fact, Satan probably didn't think much of them at all that day–certainly not enough to warrant turning his attention away from his grander scheme against mankind. Some things in this life are as they are, and some things happen as the result of our own human neglect and error. The devil knows he is on a clock and that his time is short for accomplishing what he is trying to do. If the air is out of your tires and your power is shut off, most of the time those are the results of not taking care of your car and paying your bills on time.

Then there are those who feel their years of service and time, or the amount of money they have given has earned them a special place in the Kingdom. They believe these acts have earned them some clout in Gods eyes. Yet, it is not the sacrifice alone that honors God. What good is a physical sacrifice if our hearts do not fall into obedience with God? Some think they cannot be touched by the judgment of sin because of what they "Do," but the enemy is not afraid of your sacrifice. The Prophet Samuel tells King Saul in 1 Samuel 15:22, after Saul didn't follow the Lords instructions, "To obey is better than sacrifice." Saul did what he thought was right. He allowed his position to cloud his judgment and did what he thought made sense, but Samuel called what Saul did "evil in the eyes of God." **(15:19)**

Paul, in the New Testament, warns the church in Corinth of a tactic of the enemy when it came to "Forgiving the Sinner:"

"The reason I wrote you was to see if you would stand the test and be obedient in everything. If you forgive anyone, I also forgive him. And what I have forgiven—if there was anything to forgive—I have forgiven in the sight of Christ for your sake, in order that Satan might not outwit us. For we are not unaware of his schemes." Corinthians 2:9-11 (NIV)

Paul alludes to the fact that one tactic of Satan is to get the church to operate in un-forgiveness. He mentions in verse 11 that Satan has "schemes." Many people believe that studying the devil is pointless, but the Bible speaks of him and his abilities for a reason. We cannot fight our enemy unless we know who our enemy is. How can we resist him if we are unaware of how he will tempt us? When two forces face each other in war, the advantage one would have over his enemy, is his knowledge of the enemy. They learn about the opponent's armor and weapons, his weaknesses and strengths. It's like getting your hands on the playbook of a rival football team. Having possession of that book gives you access to all their moves and strategies. Believers, we have been given the playbook of the enemy, and it is God's Word.

I learned the following verse as a child:

"The thief comes ONLY to steal and kill and destroy; I have come that they may have life, and have it to the full." John 10:10 (NIV)

Satan does not show up unless it is to do one or even all of these things. When the enemy shows up it's not just to give us a bad day. We must figure out what is threatening him, and why he would attempt to steal, kill or destroy it.

My brother spent available moments teaching me about Christ and about how to come against the enemy. Those lessons are for another book. The kingdom of the enemy shakes when a believer is armed with the knowledge God. That day war was waged against my family because the curtain was pulled away and the enemy was exposed.

That day I became wiser. I still had plenty to learn, but I was no longer in the dark. I would not allow fear to torment me anymore. I saw God now through "Big Girl Eyes," and I understood now that there was an enemy who did not want me to have peace, victory, and hope.

THIS WAS MY GOD

My father left his job as a security officer a little before James had arrived in America. He went into business for himself transporting people back and forth along the bus routes in a brand new van he and my mother had purchased. He was making a decent living that way and made a lot of friends who were doing the same thing. Most New Yorkers knew them as "Dollar Van Drivers." They were cheaper than the busses and most of the time faster. (And, no, they were not legal; not until much later anyway.) The friends my father drove around with were all Jamaicans and they pretty much all drank, smoked cigarettes and weed, and gambled by playing different card and dice games with each other. They were not the best of influences around us.

The bond between James and my father grew stronger as time went by. James would later tell me that one time my father shared with him why he couldn't let his guard down with his kids. He felt that if he showed us any form of affection or friendship we would take advantage of him and he would lose control. That's why he was so strict with us and kept his distance.

James also got to know many of my dad's friends and associates. One of my father's friends, we will call him Bruce , was always over our house. My mother was not too fond of him because he was vulgar and rude. One day my mother was on the van and a call came over the CB radio from one of the other drivers. The driver must have said something smart because Bruce grabbed the radio and started cursing out the other driver. He threatened to kill him and do a lot of other things to the man. My mother warned my father he was bad news and she didn't want Bruce around him, or us. My dad did not comply with her wishes and would meet with him secretly. If Bruce showed up when we were out with our father, my dad made us promise we would not tell her.

Another day my father picked up Bruce, who stayed with him on his run. My dad made about $80 that day and put it under the mat of his van. My father needed to run an errand, so he left Bruce waiting for him in the van. When my dad dropped him off after running his errand, he checked under the mat and the money was gone. He knew right away that Bruce had taken the money so he went to the police and reported it. This news spread throughout the other van drivers, but no one said anything because my father was seriously feared among them.

He was not one to be messed with and everyone knew that. Let me give you some examples of why he was so feared. An incident occurred that I will not forget. Peter was sleeping in the front seat and my dad had a few of his friends in the back row of his van when a homeless woman came to the window asking for money. His friends laughed at her and cursed at her. My father laughed at her and rolled up the window and drove off. He only drove a few feet before having to stop at a stoplight. My father did not see that the homeless lady was running after the van. She tried to open the other doors to get at his friends who insulted her. When she couldn't, she opened the door where Peter was sleeping, pulled him out on the floor and started climbing in the van to go after my father's friend. My dad got out of the van, dragged her out and proceeded to beat her up in the street. Several people watched as he kicked and stomped on this woman and no one interfered. The other drivers, as they drove by, saw him and just laughed because they knew that was who he was.

Another time, my father's van was broken into and someone stole the CB radio. He got a call about a man who was selling his radio not far from where we lived. The man did not realize who my father was and tried to sell it back to him. My father went into his car, got his crowbar and beat the man an inch from death. The wretched man with whom I lived at home was worse in the streets. You know the saying, "his bark is worse than his bite." Well that was far from the truth with him. My father's bite was far worse than his bark, and if you survived, you had the scars to remember the attack.

So in hearing that Bruce stole from dad, the van drivers knew my dad would not let this go so easily.

In June of 1991, the van drivers were having a block party and asked my father to cook something for the party. At the same time, my church started a van service for the youth on Friday nights as well. James really thought of staying behind to be with my father, but he decided to come along with me instead. We had a wonderful time that Friday, but something just didn't seem right the moment we arrived back at our apartment building. We walked to our building where we were met by the wife of one of my father's friends.

"Did you hear about your father?" She asked.

"No," James responded with confusion.

"Well he finally got what he deserved!"

What did that mean? James and I didn't really think twice about it, we just went upstairs. No one was home. My mom was gone along with Peter and my dad. We checked the answering machine and there was a message from my mother. She explained that my father had been shot. James dropped on the bed as he listened to the message. I was in the room, but everything went silent. It was like a bomb had gone off and I lost my hearing. I didn't know what to think. Was this really happening?

We called our youth leader, Pastor Daniel, and told him what happened. My brother wanted answers; we still did not know how or why this happened. Pastor Dan showed up minutes before my mother walked in the door herself. She was in a state of shock and disarray. She explained that my father was not dead and that he was still in the hospital. She came home to make sure we were okay and then she was going back to the hospital. She explained to us that shortly after we left to go to youth group, my father finished making soup for the party and drove to the place where it was being held.

The following is what eye witnesses said happened. . .

Everyone, including Bruce was standing outside. The music was blasting like at any other party, but this one was a set up. All of my father's friends had turned on him and made up this fake party. They knew he loved cooking for these parties and that he would definitely show up to socialize or at least drop off the food. As soon as my dad drove up the block, Bruce started screaming vulgarities at him. He yelled out that my dad was finally going to get what he deserved. My father continued to drive up, but he never shut off the van. He rolled down the window and started arguing back and forth with Bruce. The argument got so ridiculous that they eventually started spitting in each other's faces.

Bruce then pulled out a gun and shot my father. The bullet landed directly in his throat. After getting shot, my father put the van into drive and tried to drive off, but Bruce stood right in front of my dad's van. I don't know why he didn't run him over. Thinking of it now, it was clear that God was taking over. Bruce pulled the trigger a second time and tried to shoot through the windshield at my father, but the gun jammed. This gave my father enough time to back up and drive off. It was then that his gun started working again and he proceeded to shoot up the van as my dad sped off.

Now if you're thinking, "Oh, he got grazed," you are mistaken. The bullet went in through the left side of his neck and exited on the right. I have to tell you that if I was not around to hear this story, I would think it was totally impossible. According to the report filed, my father proceeded to drive down the road in the OPPOSITE direction of traffic. He drove for about a mile or so until he arrived at a police station. He passed out as the officers surrounded the van. My father had stuck two fingers in the bullet holes which bought him extra time and helped him breathe. One of the police officers ran outside as an ambulance just happened to be driving by and they rushed him to the hospital. I know . . . crazy – but that's the story HE told us.

My father was a horrible, foul mouthed, abusive, drunkard who would kill you if you looked at him wrong. Yet, God saw him as a hurt soul who needed to be saved. God performed an absolute miracle just to give my dad a chance to be saved. God did it even though He knew the type of man my father was. To me, this is love in its purest form. Jesus didn't save my father because he was the biggest giver in the church or because he was the world's greatest dad. He was definitely not a man after God's own heart. My father wasn't father of the year or the perfect model citizen. This was Jesus, the Good Physician, who came for the sick, not only for the healthy. This was, and is, the kind of God I serve.

Sometimes this characteristic of God is hard for some to understand. We feel we should have a say in what happens to those that abuse and persecute us. We think any form of kindness or mercy towards them would be unjust and unfair. The truth is, God knew that if my dad were to enter eternity he would have gone straight to hell.

"The Lord is not slow in keeping his promise, as some understand slowness. Instead he is patient with

you, not wanting anyone to perish, but everyone to come to repentance." 2 Peter 3:9 (NIV)

This kind of mercy is absolutely wonderful if it is being shown to us, but when it comes to our enemies and those who break us down, we think this must be some defect in God's make- up and judgment. What is actually God's mercy and grace – we label injustice and unfair judgment.

I would love to say I saw it as mercy and grace at age thirteen. I surely did not. Me? I was angry he had survived. What was God thinking? Didn't he know what I had been going through? This was finally my chance at freedom and a real life. It was like the end of Jonah's story. He didn't want God to spare the Ninevites. Knowing that God would be merciful and not punish those miserable people made Jonah angry. Yeah, that's what I was pretty much feeling at that moment.

While I dealt with my issues, my older brother went through a time of reflection. When the van was returned to us it had blood everywhere. I never saw it, but James told me about it. He looked at the blood stains and played the story back in his mind. The bullet that exited my father's throat went to the passenger's side and made an indentation on the frame. If my brother had gone that night he would have been in that seat, and dead for sure. God protected my brother.

To make matters more intense, we found out later that Bruce was a wanted man in another state. He had murdered someone and it was rumored he had cut up the man and threw him in a lake. He was hiding from the law which explained why it was such a big deal that my father went to the police.

My father had to be assigned a different name in the hospital because there were reports that Bruce wanted to finish the job even if it meant going to the hospital to do it. I went to school the following Monday. In the middle of the day I was asked to gather all my things and to report to the office. James was there to pick me up. Apparently Bruce ended up getting a message to my dad in the hospital. Bruce told him if he could not get to him in the hospital, he would go after his family. He told my father which school Peter and I attended and the bus my mother rode. He even told him the route we took to go to school.

We all went home that day and were given strict instructions on how to walk home and what not to do. Remember my conversation with God when I first got saved? He told me I would not make it without Him that year. That all came back to me. I don't know what the outcome was supposed to be, but my testimony now is that I am still here. Bruce was not able to get either of us. I am not sure if he even tried, but with his criminal record, it would have been foolish to think he was bluffing.

<u>WHY?</u>

God began dealing with me and I started to worry about my dad. The doctors made it very clear to my mother that my father should not have lived. The damage was extensive and there was a lot of reconstructive work that needed to be done on him. The bullet shattered his wind pipe and his voice box, but if there was any safe place a bullet could go into a person's throat and live, that's where it went for my father. The bullet missed every vital organ and that's why he was able to survive.

We went to the hospital sometime that week and waited for what seemed like forever to see him. They would not let all three of us in at one time along with my mother. I became increasingly impatient. I said, "What are we here for?" I meant it like, "Come on, we're here to see our father, not wait in some stupid room." James thought I was saying, "Why did we come to see our father?" He was so angry and started to yell at me a bit. I didn't really care to explain myself, so I let him think what he wanted.

A few minutes later, we were told to wait outside the hallway and to look down the corridor. I will never forget standing there, looking down the hall and seeing my father in his hospital gown hooked up to every machine you could think of. He was weak and needed my mom to help him walk. Since we could not come to see him, he decided to step out of the room to see us. I didn't appreciate that at the moment, but as I type it now, I am broken and unable to see the keys because of the tears. After years of not seeing one real act of love from him, he made up for it by taking those tiny steps towards us. The nurse ended up letting us all go in and we were allowed to spend some time with him. He was unable to speak, but just being with him was all the medicine he needed at that moment.

Friday, one week after the shooting, as we were about to get in the elevator to go to youth group, the doors opened and there stood my mother and father. God continued to do miracles because one week after my father was shot directly in the throat he was released and came home. Personally, I don't think they released him because they wanted to, I think he left because he didn't want to be there any longer. I wish I could say I was happy, but I was not as excited as my brother who saw the miracle in all of it. I thought otherwise. Even though he was home, he had a long road ahead of him, but ultimately my father made a full recovery.

Shortly after, the police managed to arrest Bruce . Bruce had called the house telling my father he would eventually kill him. When they found him they deported him back to Jamaica where he was to serve time. We never heard from him again.

My father's brush with death left him rethinking his life and he started reading the Bible. On many occasions, I came home to see my father reading the Word. Apparently this started in the hospital because there was a Bible in the drawer next to his bed and he would read it when he was alone. I was happy. I thought to myself he was actually changing. I wanted to believe he was different.

One day I was home with my father and Peter when someone rang the doorbell. My dad was sleeping in the bedroom so I answered it. I didn't open the door because I was taught to never open it no matter what. At the door was one of father's best friends who had been looking for him. Now at that time, I was unaware of over half the things I just shared with you, so responding to who was at the door was no big deal to me. When my father woke up I told him about his friend coming to the door. I thought I did the right thing by not opening it, but I was wrong. Apparently, I should have not even responded at all and said nothing.

My father became enraged and I did not know why. Barely able to move and talk he came up to my face and grabbed me by the shirt and actually started beating me. "Are you serious right now," I thought. He hadn't changed – he was the same man he was before and I started wishing he had died even more now. Every foul word I could think of came to my head.

"You saved him just for him to continue doing this to me? Why?"

My brother saw things differently. He grew to love my father more and was still holding a grudge against me for my comment at the hospital. I even resented James for yelling at me that way. I didn't mean it the way he took it, but I wanted him to keep thinking I did. I was fine with that and even proud of it because I hated my father so much.

James love for my father grew from the times they continued to have with each other. He told me of different accounts when he and my dad talked about personal things.

My father confessed a lot of his shortcomings and their bond grew stronger. My father worked to give up smoking and drinking for personal reasons, and because his throat could not handle those things anymore. He got rid of all his friends because, well, they were all willing to let him die. None of them thought he was going to survive, but when he did they had no excuse for siding with Bruce or for not even visiting him after his hospital stay. One by one the friends disappeared and my dad was by himself – replacing them with James .

Life started changing in a good way. The drama behind my father's shooting eventually died down. Despite his irritation towards me for my comment months ago, James and I still absolutely loved each other's company. We shared the responsibilities of cleaning the house and taking care of Peter . We had many laughs and did everything together. We played video games, did our chores with one another and kept each other in good spirits.

Several times after school was done, James would be outside the gate waiting for me and together we would go pick up Peter . On the days he did not meet me, I would make a fast dash home just so we could do something fun. I hated it when he had to get a job, but even then we had fun. He taught me as much as he could. Every day was a new lesson of some sort.

Around this time, God added another person to my story. Pastor Dan and his wife felt it was best to move on to a new church. I was hurt, but God brought another youth pastor whose name was Pastor Jonathan. He was brought in to shake up my youth group and the church a bit. He would not play a part in my life until a little later, but this man would help to give me the thing I had been missing out on for years.

¿

Chapter 9

HATE IS A STRONG WORD

The first few months my father worked hard to change and live a different life. He actually came to church with us a few times. I prayed many times when my pastor would ask if anyone wanted to give their heart to the Lord that my father would be the one to raise his hand and walk up for prayer, but it didn't happen.

Just when I thought life was becoming normal, things were stirred up again. I was in 8th grade now and even though things were still a little crazy at school, it wasn't anything too drastic. God had been working in me and I was not doing half the bad things I did before. I was struggling with one of my teachers. She was extremely mean and very nasty to me. When I told my mother, she called the teacher and spoke with her. The conversation apparently resulted in an argument between them. Now my father had to go up to the school to have a meeting with the teacher. She complained about my behavior and my attitude. To my father it seemed I was the same out of control, disrespectful girl he had to discipline a year ago. I tell you this, my friend – I was a different girl. My father didn't believe it though, so he told me when school was over I was to go to her office and apologize. So that's what I did.

When all my classes were done I went to her office, but she was not there. I looked for her (truth be told I did not look for her as hard as I should have), but she was not around. So I started on my way home. When I got home James and my dad were there. My father asked me immediately if I had done what he said and I told him she was not there. No belt this time. He started questioning me. My answers were not soothing his growing anger. Without me expecting it, he grabbed me and threw me in my room, slapping me repeatedly in the face. When I fell on the bed, he got on top of me and started to punch me in my mouth.

He lifted his fist to hit me again, but I screamed for him to please stop and that I would do it tomorrow. He got off me and left the room. He walked by my room a few times and called me a liar and screamed vulgarities to me. Each time he accused me of something bad or called me a name I would say to myself, "I am not that girl anymore." I cried not because of the blows, but because I knew I had not done anything to deserve this. I was not the person he thought I was anymore.

The phone rang. It must have been one of my friends from school because all I heard my dad say was, "No she can't come to the phone because she is a (bleep-bleep)," and then he hung up. Now I was humiliated because I didn't know which friend it was. The last thing I needed was for it to spread all over school. I didn't want to relive that again. I had finally left the other school and the stories of me being beaten at home and in school were far behind me. I worried about which friend it was that called.

My brother stayed in the kitchen and came in after it was over. I didn't really know what to expect from him. I was so embarrassed so I just sat there in silence. I was so thankful for him at that moment. I felt very choked up. I remember the moment well. In the months that passed since James came and joined us, I had not been hit once – this was the first time. The situation stirred up James' own memories. He leaned over to me and reassured me he did not think I deserved it or thought it was funny. He sympathized with me and was broken to hear those words spoken by my father again after so many years. The only difference was that this time they were said to me. He just comforted me and prayed for me. What a difference that made for me. God is so amazing – he knew what I needed.

My mom came home to see that I had been beaten up, and for the first time in a long time she stood up for me.

"You should have never hit her! Why would you hit her? I told you this woman was nasty to me! She did not deserve to get hit."

My father tried to explain himself, but my mother was not hearing it. He was remorseful for what he did, but he didn't know how to say sorry. So he just left the house for a little while. I saw it as a moment of vindication – a way in which God came to my rescue.

My mouth was still swollen when I went to school the next day. I had to make up a story, but I didn't know which of my friends had called. None of them made mention of it either. I decided to let it go. But then I thought to myself, if it wasn't someone from school then it must have been someone from my church. I never found out who it was that called until much later in my thirties. It was a friend from school, but she kept quiet about it and kept it a secret. In all those years she never alluded to anything. Through the years, without me knowing it was her that called, she remained one of my best and dearest friends.

THE BEGINNING OF FATE

I want to share a story with you that won't seem important until much later. That summer, Peter and I went to day camp. We absolutely loved it, and in more ways than one. It was a time for us to play outside for hours and do crafts. We met a lot of kids. It was such a change of pace from what we were used to.

One day, they wanted to get to know the campers, so they gave us what was called "Share Time." We were supposed to get up and tell something about ourselves, so I decided to tell about my father almost dying a few months earlier. I told them he was shot in the throat by a guy who robbed him and wanted revenge. I went on to tell them about the shooting and how the man had been on the loose but was caught and arrested. The strange thing was that the camp director knew about these events.

"Oh, I heard that story. Your father was robbed at gun point and shot in the neck, right?" she said.

"Yeah, but how did you know that?" I answered puzzled.

"It was on the news."

"It was?" I asked.

"Yeah the man who robbed your father was Jamaican, right? He got away and they were looking for him."

"Yeah." My father was on the news – the news – I thought.

"Your father is white right? And he died?"

"No, my father is Jamaican too and he lived," I said confused.

"Really?" She said. "The news said this man died."

I was absolutely baffled. Why would they say my dad died? I went home and told my mom who said my father was never on the news, so I brushed it off. This moment will turn out to be one of the biggest God moments ever. But you have to wait for that.

THE AWKWARD MOMENT

Shortly after the last incident with my father, I started to pray more for my mom (Now this is a part of my testimony many people have had problems hearing. I tell you the truth I am not making this up). As I prayed for her, God told me, "You're mother is not going to give her life to me until someone she cares about passes away." I saw it as a statement about sacrifice, but it wasn't. God knew my mom was not going to turn to Him unless something rocked her world drastically. Nevertheless, I felt this was finally my opportunity to plead for God to take my life. I waited until a night James worked really late and started praying God would take me in my sleep.

I didn't want to live anymore. I couldn't live this life any longer. I loved James, but the pain from the past was still too much. I saw that my life at home was changing and getting better, but I didn't want to see another day. I knew in my heart that what God spoke concerning my mother was true, so I wrote a note to my family believing God would take me in order for my mother to get saved. I was so excited, and yet I was sad at the same time because I didn't really get to tell my family how I loved them.

I went to sleep ready for the end. I cannot explain my emotions when I woke up the next day. I was so angry. I was extremely disappointed. Silently, because the boys were still asleep, I began to weep.

"How could you do this?" I said. "Don't you understand I don't want to be here anymore? Don't you understand my mother is not going to get saved until tragedy hits?"

I cried and cried unable to contain myself because I wanted to die. After calming down, I felt God speak.

"I have a greater plan for you. I am going to use you to touch many. You are too valuable to lose, my child."

"What about my mother?" I asked.

"There will be a loss, but it cannot be you."

He had a calling for me? What did that mean? I didn't tell James what I asked God for. I ripped up the letter and went on believing that God had this mysterious calling on my life, whatever that meant.

Months later I had a dream. In the dream I was floating in the air in a hospital and everyone was crying. I could see through the walls and I saw my mother crying hysterically. I looked to see who was in the bed? It was my father! He was dead in the hospital bed. "How is that possible," I thought, "He just survived a bullet wound?" I heard God say, "One day your father will be there and the next he will be gone." I woke up from the dream all out of sorts. What did this mean? I went to James , who was in the kitchen, and told him exactly what I saw.

"I just had the weirdest dream. I dreamt that dad died."

"How is that possible when God just saved his life almost 10 months ago?" He said to me angrily. "That's ridiculous!"

I had had some arguments with James since he had joined us from Jamaica, but he never shot me down like that before. He started rebuking me and telling me I didn't know what I was talking about because God would not save dad to allow him to die almost one year later. I walked away and never spoke of it again to him.

During all this time, I was getting close to Pastor Jon, so I decided to share the dream with him. He brushed me off the exact same way my brother had, just not as bad. Maybe I was wrong. I tried to forget it, but I know what I heard the Lord say and it kept echoing in my head, "One day your father will be there and the next he will be gone." My spirit knew something was coming even though I tried to put away the dream.

YOUTH CONVENTION

In April of 1992, I had an encounter with God I could not have dared predict. As they did every year, my youth group prepared to go away to a youth convention in Syracuse, New York. I had never ever gone away, so I didn't think my parents would let James and I go. To make it worse, James later told me he would not be able to go, so I had to ask if I could go alone. Amazingly my father said yes. Again, what I found crazy about my dad was that no matter how much he beat me and punished me, he never ever stopped me from going to church, ever.

Two weeks or so before I went on this trip, my dad gave me my first real Bible (Weird, I know, just wait). Someone left it in his van. It was a beautiful red leather Bible with gold edging. I absolutely loved it, and I brought it with me on the trip.

When the day came for us to leave our church to go to Syracuse, I felt like I was leaving home and that I wasn't going to return the same. The whole thing was so wonderful. I was able to get to know my new youth leader much better. He was wonderful and fun loving. The first night, the arena we met in was filled with over 4,000 teens from all over the state. It was the most amazing moment I had ever had.

The atmosphere was thick with God's presence. When the worship started, hundreds of young people ran to the main floor and worshipped at the stage where the band played. I was too scared to leave because I didn't know if I would get lost so I stayed with one of my close friends at church.

I can't remember what the preacher spoke about that night, like always, but I listened intensely. I already knew that once the altar call was made I was going to step out in faith and go. Other members of my youth group followed as I went, but it wasn't about them, it was about me getting closer to God. I went to the altar, which was just a dirty floor at the bottom of the arena, but as I approached it, I felt Jesus was waiting for me. I had never felt the presence of God the way I did at that moment. I could not contain myself as a flood of emotion filled me. What was this? I broke down crying as I realized this was the pure love of God wrapping around me.

God made himself real to me on another level at that moment. I cried so hard that I ended up on that dirty floor

155

weeping. I was a broken mess. I had never felt so much love at one time. At that moment, I felt a hand on my shoulder and it picked me up off the floor. It was Pastor Jonathan . He was once a football player, and he wrapped his huge arms around me and I just broke down more. I had never ever been hugged like that with such purity and love in all my life. Just thinking of that moment now makes me break down in tears.

There was a long awaited release that flowed through me. I didn't need any words, I needed affection and love. Pastor J stepped through this massive group of teens worshipping, found me at the altar and became the physical arms of Jesus for me. He had no idea I was an abused child or that I was at the end of my rope wanting to die every day. I was so desperate for a change in my life and that weekend was the beginning of things changing. I left that weekend a changed girl. I was not going to do things the same way and I promised God I would trust Him more through the trials of my life.

THE RUG PULLED OUT FROM UNDER ME

Like many teens who have an amazing time at Convention, I did not look forward to coming back home. It was painful to do, but I felt God really loved me and I took that with me. I was more confident and braver, especially with James there. Everything was so much better now that he was with me. I couldn't wait to tell him what had happened. James was in the bedroom and he had news too, but he let me go first. I told him everything that happened over the weekend. He listened patiently and eagerly to hear the details of my experiences.

After telling him everything, he announced to me his news. He had signed up for the military and would be leaving to join the Marine Corps in a matter of weeks. I felt all the blood leave my face. It was like I had been punched in the stomach. He had signed up while I was gone and was going to be leaving in less than a month. How could he do this to me? How could he leave me like this? Didn't he know how much I loved him and needed him? I begged him not to leave, but it was final. I didn't say anything else to him.

I was not expecting this. Looking at it now, I see that my experience at Convention helped prepare me, not just for this news, but also for the year to come. I see that God was trying to build me up for what I would have to face when I returned home. I don't know what I would have done if I had not gone away and had that experience with God, probably gone through with a suicide attempt.

James' last few days with us were very hard. He was a physical sign for me of safety and the fear of that being gone crushed me. Things were different since he came to live with us. He changed our home for the better. Now it was going to go back to the way it was before, when I was doing every-thing and the beatings would return. I became very bitter and resentful toward him with every passing day. I only spent one year with him and now he was leaving. He couldn't do this another time? It didn't matter now. He was getting ready for boot camp and would be back in six weeks before being stationed.

<u>PETER</u>

After James left I went through some depression but life was not as bad as it was before. One of the thing James taught me was the power of worship. He introduced me to a ton of different worship albums. On many occasions I would put on those songs and soaked in God's presence. I was too addicted to God to forget Him in this serious time of my life. When I went to church it was the same thing. I knew the same God who was at Convention was also the God who met me at church. Sometimes I couldn't wait for the message to be over so I could find a spot at the altar, right next to the piano, and just leave another broken piece of myself there. I was allowed to cry openly here at church and I took advantage of that since I couldn't do it at home. This act soon became contagious as many of the other teens from my church began joining me in the front at the altar.

At home, I needed to fix things with Peter . Truth be told, when James showed up, Peter took a back seat. Before that it was Peter, my buddy, my companion. We played together, fought with each other and got into trouble together. I didn't do things with him the same way that we used to.

Before James , my father would leave Peter and me alone at home and we would have adventures and pretend sessions lasting for hours. We would turn our room into a camping area or a house. We took every sheet we had and tacked or hammered them to the wall, leaving tons of tiny holes. Then we'd gather some food from the fridge and spend the day pretending we were stranded on an island or a boat. Daisy, our cat, who was actually a boy (don't ask) was either the shark or bear, depending on the location.

Daisy would play along with us strangely enough. He would hide under our bed and wait for us to put our foot in view and try to swat at us. If you were tagged by Daisy you would pretend he was dragging you under and the other person would have to pull you back up to safety. Most of the time, I don't know why, it was Peter who was mauled by the bear or shark and I would have to be the one dragging him to safety.

On other days, when we were by ourselves, we would pretend I was doing a cooking show – I was the cook and he would be operating the camera. We had commercials and sometimes guest stars would have to taste the new recipe. I would create all these different dishes, and again, faithful Peter had to taste test everything (He survived that too, he was a strong boy).

On another occasion we pretended to be a couple on the TV show called *Solid Gold*. That was sort of the 80's version of "*So You Think You Can Dance*," for you younger readers. I would be the guy, because I had to lead the dances of course, and Peter would be the girl. To make it more realistic, I would put him in my old dresses and twirl him around.

I got in trouble one time when I twirled him around way too much and he became dizzy. He slipped and dislocated his shoulder. Still, other times, I would take my mother's makeup and draw mustaches and eyebrows on him.

I didn't realize it until he told me later, but Peter missed those moments with me when James showed up. He truly missed being mauled by our feline bear/shark, eating my disgusting recipes, wearing my mother's eyeliner and dislocating his arm during our dance-offs, which by the way, we always won – we were great.

So we reconnected and surprisingly enough it wasn't hard at all. I didn't have to do everything myself as I did before James came. Peter had watched James closely and helped me with the chores every time. He helped me finish everything faster so we could play video games together. It was still hard taking care of him, but not the way it used to be. He was a big help and he never left me alone. James called occasionally, but my talks with him were limited. I was still angry and had nothing to say to him. He abandoned me and it wasn't okay.

A STRONG REMINDER

That summer was very full. James left for the Marines, Peter and I reconnected, my relationship with God grew stronger, and I began my first summer job. Everything was new and all appearances of my old life seemed to be fading away. Then, of course, there was still my father.

One day my dad was taking a nap while Peter and I played video games. I told Peter it was time for dinner, so I dished out his dinner and we both ate as fast as we could so we could go back to playing. I made sure to wash all the dishes because I didn't want to get in trouble once my father woke up. We went back to playing and my father woke up. Quickly, out of impulse, I went through a check list in my mind, making sure I had done everything my father had asked.

Shortly after, my father went into the kitchen and called for Peter to come. I waited for him to come back, but instead minutes later my dad called me. When I looked, Peter was at the table eating again. My father asked me if I had fed him and I told my dad I did. Apparently, my father had asked my brother if he was hungry and Peter was too scared to say, "No." My dad gave him another plate of food and that's when he called me out. Now, Peter was confused about my father's question. In the past he had been spanked for saying "No" when it came to food that he was offered. In my culture, it can be considered an insult to reject food when it is offered. I wasn't upset with him at all. I knew he was eating because he was scared. But now I had to defend myself.

I told my father I had already fed him, but he didn't believe me because there were no plates in the sink to show it. The more I tried to defend myself the angrier he got. He finally took the broom next to him, grabbed me by the shirt and cornered me between the front door and him. He held the broom like a bat and was about to bash me in my head with the handle. At that very moment I prayed to myself, "God, if you are in Heaven you need to stop him! He is surely going to kill me now!" In mid swing my father stopped when he saw Peter's face.

My brother was mortified and he showed it in his face, so my father put the broom down and stared back at me for several seconds.

"I'm going to kill you, but not today. Not yet."

He went back to the kitchen and kept his eyes on me. He was serious. He was not playing or being dramatic.

"I've told you this before; you play a lot of games. You play games with your mother, but you're not going to play games with me. You want to play games, then let's play, but you have to know this, I always win. I have never lost a game." He looked me directly in the face and said, "I will kill you."

He had so much confidence after surviving a bullet to the neck and I knew he was serious. Surprisingly, I didn't get as scared so much as angry. I refused to be scared or timid or the victim any longer. I had enough! Yes, my life was new and God helped give me new purpose, but one thing still remained in me, anger. I was tired of living this way and I was not going to cower any longer. I told God, "If you do not kill this man, I PROMISE YOU, I will." I was just as serious as my father. I was not threatening God, I was promising him. I was not going to live one more day like this, not anymore.

I heard nothing from God in response.

I later found out I was not the only one who hated my father. That same day, at the age of seven, Peter was not going to let my father kill me. My little brother told me many years later he was aiming to kill our father before he could kill me. He told me that after he heard our dad say that to me he started sleeping with a knife under his mattress. Many nights my father would come into our room to make sure that we were okay. Peter said he was hoping my dad would come close enough into the room so he could stab him.

I also discovered that I was not the only one who had wished my father died when he was shot. Peter explained to me that he believed we would finally be free from him once he heard he was in the hospital. Now, since my dad did not die, this little seven year old boy felt he would have to end his dad's life in order to protect his big sister.

Thankfully, Peter was not given the opportunity. My parents began prepping to see James in California where he was stationed for his graduation. They would be gone for at least four days, but because of my summer job I was not able to go. I was so happy. I did want to see my big brother, despite my anger towards him, but the last thing I wanted was to be with my father.

Days later James arrived. He was the most handsome Marine I had ever seen. He was not dressed in his suit, but you could tell he was stronger, wiser and grown up. I ran to him, we hugged and I almost cried. Oh man had I missed him.

Like old times, we waited until it was night time and we talked for hours. There was little that was different about him towards me, but there was a lot that was different about him concerning God. Sadly, my brother was struggling to keep the values he so strongly talked to me about. To make matters worse, I didn't know when he came back that it was only for a short visit. He was soon leaving to be stationed somewhere. I tried to hide it, but it made me even angrier with him for leaving.

James brought laughter back to the house in the time he was with us. My father was a different person when he was around. His son was a Marine and he had such admiration for him. I can honestly say I had no jealousy towards my brother because he deserved it. He had shown my father he was going to make something of himself and he was not going to let this world turn him into another statistic.

I may have been happy for my dad, but I did not trust him. I still hated him and wanted nothing to do with him. In my mind this feeling was completely justified. This monster must go and I would not rest until God answered my prayers.

Chapter 10

IT HAPPENED

[The following is written down as best as can be remembered by those involved. I am in no way knowledgeable of medical terms or procedures. To those who may have experiences in the medical field, if something seems wrong in it's explanation, know that I am not glamorizing the story. I am only telling it as it was explained to me.]

July 29, 1992 was a day I will never forget. It started like any other day as I prepared to leave for my summer job. My mother left for work and my father was nowhere to be found. I got my clothes on and started my 4 block walk to the bus stop. A block and a half before I got to the stop, I looked behind me and noticed someone there, it was my father. When I moved to the side, he passed me like he was a complete stranger. No "Hi," "Have a good day," or even "Goodbye." He was carrying something on his shoulders. It looked like a part to a car.

At that moment–I know it sounds weird, but I felt the Lord say to me, "Say goodbye to your father. It's the last time you will see him." My dad turned at the corner of the sidewalk. I watched him, but I never said goodbye. I kept on walking, caught the bus and never thought twice about him. I didn't even think about the statement God made. I just went to work.

My day went well, as far as summer jobs go. In fact, I was quite proud of myself because the place where I worked was in the office of the Housing Preservation Development Department. As I walked home that day, I was thought about how blessed I was. To work there was a big deal. I wasn't anything special there, and it was just for the summer, but it was something I was proud to have.

I walked into our apartment. Something was wrong. I couldn't pinpoint it, except that things were moved around in the living room. Something happened, I knew that much, but what? I found James on my dad's bed waiting for me. I greeted him and he told me he had to tell me something.

"What?" I said.

"It's dad," he replied.

"What happened?"

He paused before he spoke, "He had a stroke..."

I don't mean this literally, but my world stood still. It stopped in mid-motion as he continued to say . . .

"... and they don't think he's going to make it."

I was in shock. I didn't know what to say or do.

This seems to be the order of events that occurred while I was at work:

After my father and I went our separate ways that morning, he was going to take a car part to be fixed just a few blocks away from where I had last saw him. At some point, he started getting a massive headache. Someone he knows found him sitting on the curb almost across from where I caught the bus. He could not explain what he was feeling, except that he was feeling weird. The man who found him knew where we lived, so he picked my dad up and took him home.

James was home with Peter. He was surprised when the man brought my father in. My father told James about the headache and went to lie down on the floor in the living room. While he was lying down, he started to complain that he was cold. My brother decided to call my mother and told her what was going on. She told James to put my father on the phone. When my dad got on the phone, my mom asked him what was wrong. All he could whisper was that he didn't know. Now my father was not a man who got sick, so for him to be complaining of anything was cause for alarm to my mom.

My mother told James to call 911 and that she would meet him at the hospital. That's exactly what my brother did. When the dispatcher asked him what was wrong, James told him his father was complaining of headaches.

James told my dad help was coming and that they were going to the hospital so my father got up and started looking for the medical cards, but he did it in such a violent way. He started yanking out drawers and pulling things apart. At some point, James had to restrain him. He became delusional, looking at James, and he was calling James, Peter. Then he just started calling out for Peter over and over again. At some point my dad started feeling more and more pain and started to freak out.

James got dad to lie down calmly and close his eyes. Shortly after, he sat up and screamed, "Oh God, I'm dead! I'm dead! I'm dead!" He saw something and started screaming and yelling. My brother tried calming him down again and told him he wasn't dead, he wasn't going to die. James started praying over him and ministering to him. A peace came over him that allowed him to rest a little. He was still in grave pain, but the peace of God kept him calm.

James told Peter to call the ambulance again because it was going on 15 minutes and they still had not arrived. Eventually, two of the maintenance men from the building came in to help James. James continued talking to him about the love and the power of Jesus. It was like my brother knew something was wrong and he wasn't going to take any chances. The peace of God continued to be on him as James prayed for him. James told Peter to call again because it was now 25 minutes and no ambulance.

The ambulance arrived 30 minutes after the initial call. Apparently they did not take the call seriously. It was a guy with a headache. They came in and asked my father several questions which he was able to answer. The elevator could not hold an ambulance bed, so my father had to stand on his two feet and walk with them downstairs.

While in the ambulance he had several mini strokes. When they brought him into the hospital they ran a few tests, then placed him to the side. They still were not taking his situation very seriously. He lay on the stretcher on the side of the ER, He kept asking to go to the bathroom, but they kept making him wait. Eventually, he got up to go to the bathroom, that's when he had a massive stroke. This stroke was so severe that it snapped his brain stem. The entire hospital seemed to stop everything they were doing to attend to him.

It was at this moment my mother showed up. She could not believe what was happening. She was not expecting to see this going on with her husband. She had just spoken to him on the phone.

The hospital was not equipped to give him the necessary testing needed, so they had to take him to another hospital in Manhattan. My mother went with them and sent Peter and James home. At the new hospital they conducted a CT scan. The test showed there was no brain activity. They conducted one more test to see the extent of the damage. This is one of the most painful tests to conduct, but it would show how bad he was. They shot freezing cold water in his ear drum to see if there was any reaction, but there was no response. It was then that they officially declared him brain dead.

This was far worse than what my mother imagined. When they allowed her to go in the room, she saw his face was completely swollen. As he lay there, she spoke to him and said jokingly, "One year later? I can't keep doing this every year." A nurse was assigned to stay with him in the room as my mom visited. The nurse could tell she wasn't getting it. She explained to my mom that he was in a bad state and that it didn't look good. She was very blunt with my mom and told her there was a great chance he would die. The doctors were not even going to attempt surgery or try and save him because the damage to his brain was already too extensive. It was now just a matter of time before he died.

My mom told me the moment the nurse said that, a tear rolled down my father's face. He may have been brain dead, but something was still alive enough to hear he wasn't going to make it.

The nurse gave my mother some private time with him and left the room.

"I just saw you this morning," she thought to herself.

She saw him at 7:15 when he made her morning tea.

They spoke on the phone at 9:45.

Now, at 11:30, he was pronounced completely brain dead.

She sat at his bedside totally unable to process this moment.

As she explained it to me, I already knew the image. This was the dream I had months before. The dream I was told was not going to happen.

No matter how much I hated him and wanted him dead, I never wanted my mom to feel what she was feeling that day. The only things keeping my father alive at that point were the machines. His body and mind were completely gone.

The doctors explained to her that it appeared he had a thin blood vessel for many years that finally erupted, he had an aneurism. They said it occurred from a blunt force to his head, maybe at a young age. When he was in the hospital a year ago from the gun shot, they could have caught it if they had done x-rays and would have been able save his life. Apparently, this blood vessel broke and the blood rushing into his brain was causing the mini strokes; and it's what also caused the massive stroke. There was so much blood entering his brain that it completely crushed it. Based on the stories my dad told him, James believed it was from the times our grandmother beat my dad in the head with objects like pots and pans.

I have been told that usually these things happen while someone is sleeping and they just pass away in their sleep, but to be awake and experience it would be one of the most painful ways to die. The doctors continued to tell her if he were to make it out of this, he would be in a vegetable state, unable to speak, walk or function. His brain had been completely crushed by the blood and there was absolutely nothing they could do to repair the damage. It was too extensive.

My father was a horrible father, but he was a wonderful husband, if you can understand that. My mother and father were the best of friends. I can honestly say I saw a very healthy marriage with them. He absolutely worshipped the ground my mother walked on. He cooked for her and surprised her with things. They argued, lived, loved and laughed with each other. He would have done anything for her. There was never any name calling among them, no threats of divorce or bad language in disputes. He was a gentleman and he treated her as if she were fine china to be placed on display.

On many occasions when were in bed late at night, if my mother even made a suggestion she was hungry, my dad would whip her up a whole meal. If she needed to go to the store, he never hesitated. He spared no expense for her. One of the other things I cherished was waking up on a Saturday morning to listen to them talk to each other for close to an hour before their day started. He was a great provider and no matter what, we never went hungry. There were those rough times, but we always had something. He did whatever he had to do to feed his family and now my mother would have to do it alone. They could barely pay the bills before his death, how was she supposed to pay them with two of her children still young?

My cousins and some other family friends came to the house while my mother was in the hospital. When my mom came home, she officially announced to everyone that my father was gone. My mom did not have to make the decision to take him off the machine – the hospital did it for her. They knew there was way too much damage done.

I was so torn with emotions. I had never seen my mother this way. It looked like she had died with my father. I felt responsible for the pain my mother was going through. I wanted to run to her and tell her I was sorry, but I knew she wouldn't understand. Yet, at the same time, I felt saved. I thought to myself, "Could God love me this much?" I knew it was a really cruel thing to think, but I also knew both of us were not going to survive this, one had to go.

I called my youth pastor and told him what happened. The words were hard to come by and all I could do was sob. This was not easy for me to process. This man was not a friend or an enemy, he was my father, and he was dead. He was supposed to be the man who would warn me about boys. The man who would walk me down the aisle one day to give me away at my wedding. You can only have one father, and my chances of having any kind of father-daughter relationship was gone with him. My future kids would never know him. He would have loved them and spoiled them. He would have been so proud to see the talents his grandchildren had and he would have laughed with them. I know in my heart he would not have done anything to hurt them as he did to me. My dad would have done anything for them. It would have been love at first sight.

I mourned, not at the loss of the man, but the loss of a dream. I needed a dad to tell me he was proud of me and that I was doing a good job. I needed him to tell me that I was beautiful. I never got the "I love you princess." This was harder than I thought it would be, this new hurt was unexpected and more painful than the abuse. Before, there might have at least been a hope for change, now it all just ends, the way it was, with no happy ending.

August 1, 1992, was the funeral for my father. I was still a bag of mixed emotions as I was greeted at the funeral home by Pastor J. He would be doing some of the ceremony because our senior pastor was away. That was okay though, there was no one else I wanted to do this more than him.

I didn't know what to say as I looked at my father's lifeless body in the casket. I saw Peter at the side with dry eyes. It was as if nothing was really affecting him. It was sad, two out of his three kids were absolutely happy he was finally gone. I remember going up to the casket, not to give my respects, but to make sure it was really him. Peter told me he had prayed for the death of my father as often as he could. We never said this to each other until we were much older.

James got up and spoke during the ceremony. He talked of how my father loved me and cared for me blah, blah, blah . . . That's all I remember. My mind totally tuned him out because I felt he was just saying what you're supposed to say at a funeral. It was okay though, I didn't care about the truth.

After the ceremony, James took some time to talk with me alone. He wanted to see how I was doing and see if I understood what he had said. He started telling me that even though our father was cruel and harsh to me, he absolutely loved me. He told me my dad was proud of me, and how he admired how I loved reading and how I worked so hard for my grades (Despite my bad behavior I always had good grades. He never got on me about that). He went on to tell me that since my father was not able to get the best education as a child, he was always pleased with me when he saw me studying.

This story should have made me happy, right? Nope, it made me angrier because I didn't know if James was lying. James showed me a letter my dad wrote to him while he was in boot camp. In the letter, he was apologizing to James for the things he had done to him. He also told him he wished he could be closer to his kids, but my father didn't want us to forget who he was.

What was I supposed to do with this information of hidden regret and hidden love? It meant nothing to me. I grew angrier and angrier. I just wanted it over; I didn't want to feel anything anymore. I didn't know where my emotions were going, I needed help. I couldn't start loving him NOW–it was too late for that. I couldn't start regretting things now. He was gone, and I had made plans to be happy after this all went away.

One night I was laying in my bed thinking. My house had the aroma of death. You could feel it when you got off the elevator. It was waiting for us every time. It was like walking in through a dark cloud. Nothing was funny, no one wanted to eat and nothing felt right. His death brought on the fear of poverty and lack. My mother was struggling to keep up with the bills because he did not have any life insurance, and the funeral home expenses were just as extensive as the hospital bills. She was so worried that she would not be able to keep up with everything.

As I lay there thinking about all this, the Lord spoke to me, "You have nothing to worry about. I will never leave you. I will be your father. I will provide for you and protect you. I will love you the way a father should love a daughter."

At that moment, I felt the presence of God swallow me up. I could not stop crying because it was like God was hugging me from the inside out. Remember when I wrote about that time at seven years old when I asked God, "If you're so loving, then why did You let my father treat me like this?" I feel He never said anything then, because of this moment. I would not have understood. That day, I felt my Heavenly Father embrace me. He held me like His princess.

One thing I have learned in the years of serving God is that He does not just take one role in our lives. He is the "I AM" for a reason. He is not just a father, provider, healer or vindicator. He can also be a teacher, comforter or judge. In the Bible, when the children of Israel were in the desert, He did not just give himself one name. I think it was because God never wants to be cooped up in a box. He never wants us to put limits on who He is and what He can do in our lives. I cannot tell you how many people I've come across who have issues and struggles, but they never think to bring them before the Lord. He looks forward to being there for us, but we have to be willing to throw away the box in which we have placed Him.

I needed a father, and God was that for me, but he also knew I needed something else. The Friday after my father's funeral, I went to youth group like always, but I showed up a little earlier. Pastor J asked if I wanted to come upstairs and eat dinner with him and his wife Claire. I thought that was nice, so I took him up on his offer. Sister Claire and Pastor Jon had a one year old daughter and Sister Claire was pregnant with their second child. As they got their family together, I stood in the kitchen and looked out the window. All of a sudden, Pastor J came in and asked me if I was okay. I lied and said, "Yes." He didn't believe me. Then all of a sudden, He wrapped his arms around me. I will never forget that day. Again, it was like God himself was hugging me. It wasn't one of those wimpy embraces. It was one of pure love and concern, and whether he knows it or not, he started my healing process with that simple act of kindness. He went on to say, "You need a father and I will be your father." That's exactly what he was.

Can I just stop right here and talk to you. If you are a leader in the church or a mentor of a teen, you may not realize the impact you could make in a kid's life by getting out of your comfort zone and loving up on your teens. As you will continue to read, you will see that this man played a major part in where I am today. I would not be here without Pastor J taking me under his wing and loving me. There could be a teen or a young adult God has placed on your heart. Don't get too caught up in yourself and your needs. Begin to ask God what the teen needs and let God use you. I know it can get overwhelming and emotional. But if you let God lead and guide you, a simple hug, an invite to a meal at a fast food place, a game of bowling, anything, can break the chains that keep young people bound. Sometimes it doesn't need to be words, let Jesus direct you on how to minister to each individual. Spend time asking God to reveal a way to minister to them. Some may be harder than others, but remember, if you spend enough time with Jesus, you begin to smell like Him.

Pastor Jonathan had the aroma of Jesus, and for the next four years he and his wife lived up to their roles in my life.

Chapter 11

I WILL NOT BE DEFEATED
❧〰❧

"For our struggle is not against flesh and blood, but against the rulers, against the authorities, against the powers of this dark world and against the spiritual forces of evil in the heavenly realms."
Ephesians 6:12 (NIV)

PULLED FROM ALL SIDES

ife at home became very challenging after the death of my father. I watched as my mother put on this "shell" of an exterior. She was strong, she held it all together, but inside she was torn and full of heartache. All the extended family members had gone home, now it was just us. It was time to face this new reality by ourselves. Our home had one less person in it now. It was a little easier to deal with while family members stayed with us for some time and kept our minds off it all. It also provided my mom with someone her age to comfort her. Now, when it was just us, the pain of death that lingered in our home was so thick you could taste it.

My mother started going to a local church regularly, which seemed to give her some comfort. I was so happy to see her going to church, but I wondered if it would make a difference. Little by little, she began to read a Bible she had. I desperately wanted to have a relationship with her. I didn't know her, and she didn't know me. Every piece of knowledge we possessed of each other were all about surface things. Now that James was back in the Marines and Peter still young, I was all she had. And in return, she was all I had.

I decided I was going to try and be the shoulder she needed to cry on. My first act was to get her a better Bible than the one she had. Her Bible was old, so I wanted to get her one a bit bigger and with larger print because she complained the lettering in her Bible was too small. Inside the Bible I enclosed a card explaining how much I wanted to have a relationship with her and that I would try to be a friend to her. My mom received the letter as well as she could in her depressed state. I made it my business to hold up to my promise.

I desperately wanted to spend quality time with her. One of the things I was never able to do with her before was play the board game Scrabble. She would come home from work and always be too tired. I'll never forget the day I was in my room when my mom called me to the living room and asked if I wanted to play Scrabble with her. I couldn't believe it. I ran frantically to get the board and tiles. We sat at the dinner table and played in complete silence. Twenty minutes into the game, I looked over at my mother and noticed tears rolling down her cheeks. She asked me to put on a particular song we had been listening too for over a month now. It was by Boyz II Men, *It's So Hard to Say Goodbye to Yesterday.*

I get so emotional, even now, when I think about those painful moments. We would literally play for hours and she would simply cry. All I could do was sit with her and be there as she mourned. There were times when she was in her room watching TV and she would call me in to sit with her, just because she didn't want to be alone. It wasn't too long after that my mother gave her life over to the Lord.

I threw myself into church as much as I could. I became addicted to attending church and being with my church friends. It provided me a sense of safety and made me feel normal. Pastor J and his wife had me over their home regularly. I would help with their children, and at times, I would just come over to have dinner with them. It was such a change of pace for me compared to my own home. In fact, the moment I would be on my way to church, it felt like I was entering a new life. The feeling of death would lift away and I would feel normal again. I was able to laugh, play and explore being me. For those moments, I didn't have to be there for my mother or have to watch my younger brother. The weights of life would be left outside the doors of the church. My problem, however, was that I would have to pick them up again when it was time to go home. Pastor J was the one who took the church van to pick up the teens for youth group. He did me the favor of picking me up first and dropping me off last. Once I stepped out of the van doors, on a few occasions, I would begin to tear up before getting to the elevator.

November of that year, my mother told me we were moving to Florida. She was hurting too much from the memories of my father within our apartment. She admitted it was overwhelming for her, and she felt this was the best thing to do. She had contacted my aunt who had taken us in when we first came to America, Matthew's mother. They had since moved to Florida and had lived there for the last 5 years. And we would follow behind them again.

I couldn't believe it. She was going to take me away from the one thing that made me happy. My church became my refuge. I connected with its leaders. Finally, I had a group of friends who did not provoke me or force me to do thing I did not want to do. This place helped change me and mold me into a better behaved young woman, and now it was all going to be taken away. I didn't know if I could take anymore, I was at the end of my rope. I had no control over any of this, I had no say in the matter. I wanted to scream at the top of my lungs. I was going to lose all my friends and church family, but most of all I was going to lose Pastor J and Sister Claire.

THE FALL RETREAT

The day after Thanksgiving I went on a retreat to Pennsylvania. Several youth groups came together from different parts of New York to this one place for three days just to worship God. The first day, I had a great time with my friends. We played basketball, cards and mingled with other groups. I was also able to speak with Sister Claire more and we grew closer.

When the last day of the retreat approached, things changed. I think I realized that within a matter of hours we would load up the vans and we would have to head back home. It didn't sit well with me. I had a great time and I laughed a lot, but nothing had changed in my mind, it just delayed the inevitable. As we were packing our bags before the last service, another youth group played a prank on my group and it upset some of the kids. The members of my group wanted to start a fight. I didn't want to be bothered with this nonsense. It was not what I needed at the moment. I needed to get away, so I left my things and walked away as the two youth groups began arguing.

I had one very close friend named Mandy who had been there for me through all my current issues. As I was walking away, she followed behind me trying to get me to stop. I didn't want to be bothered, so I screamed at her to leave me alone. I felt so bad because she didn't deserve it. She did comply with my wishes and I continued walking away.

Across from the retreat center was a huge river. Along the riverside was a little area for people to stand, so I stopped there to think. I thought to myself, "There is no way God wants me to continue in this world like this." It was at that moment that I felt it was time to end it all.

What use was it to keep going? My logic was . . .

1) My father was dead and I was still a broken mess.
2) I wanted my older brother, but he left me.
3) I wanted a relationship with my mother, but she was too broken to be what I needed her to be.
4) I felt I couldn't take on the responsibility of caring for my little brother alone.
5) My church was the only thing I had that helped me feel like I could function, but now that was going to be taken away.
6) My church friends were like family to me, but they were currently arguing about something stupid and had no idea how much they meant to me.

I had no control over anything. This was not going the way I thought it would. I wanted out, and if God wasn't going to take me out of this world, then I would take myself out.

This is what Ephesians 6:12 was talking about. My father was dead, but I was still battling so many things. His death didn't free me from my struggles as I thought it would. I was never fighting against my father, nor was I was fighting against flesh and blood. I was fighting against "rulers, authorities, powers of the dark world and against spiritual forces of evil in the heavenly realm." This is what all God's children are battling. I had never felt such strong oppression from the enemy in all my years as I did that day.

This retreat center was located in the mountains of Pennsylvania, and though it was November, the water in the river had already frozen over in certain places. I put my hands on the railing of the dock and thought about jumping off into the icy waters. I figured I would either drown or freeze to death because no one was around to find me. I reasoned with myself how this was my best way out, and that it was not going to get any better. I continued to think this was better than any other solution, because if I did succeed, at least I would finally be able to get some rest. I truly thought my father's death would have ended all my troubles, but it just made them worse. Now I had no one to pin the blame on for my screwed up life. I alone had to face all these demons within me and I had no one to lean on.

When was I supposed to have peace? Yes, I went to the altar and gave my life to the Lord. But it was just blow after blow, and with every hit, I needed to fight that much harder. All that came to my mind was everything I was going to face at home. I couldn't, I was too tired and too worn out to fight anymore. I just wanted to sleep and shut my brain off. This was my solution.

At that moment, a girl and a guy from another church were walking by and saw me standing along the dock. They must have noticed that something wasn't right with me because the girl asked if I was okay.

"No, I can't take it anymore. I am sick of this life. I just can't go on anymore," I explained. I began to verbally run through all the mess I was feeling as the girl slowly approached me. She didn't pretend to understand, she just listened to everything and slowly placed her hand on my back. I wept. Part of me felt it was meaningless to tell her anything and that I should just go ahead and jump. My mind was telling me she couldn't help me, so why waste my energy telling her all this. After hearing everything, she simply responded by telling me there was one more service. She said that maybe God would give me an answer to my questions. She asked me to go back with her to the service. I wasn't interested in going to church and listening to another message, but after thinking about it, I went with her and her friend anyway.

I followed her back to where the service was being held. As we walked into the gym where the service was being held, my eyes caught a glimpse of a young man who seemed way taller than all the other teens. I had seen all the other kids at the retreat throughout the weekend, but this one seemed different. For this brief moment, even though I was in an awkward state at the time, my attention was drawn to him.

I sat with Mandy . She didn't say anything about me yelling at her, and I didn't say anything to her. As I sat there, I truly didn't care what the preacher was saying. No one could explain to me why I felt the pain going through me at that moment. The only thing that made sense to me was that I needed to go to the altar and plead with God. It wasn't about anything else but pure desperation. When the time came for the alter call, I went up and spoke to God.

"I am hurting. I can't do this much longer. I need you to help me on this journey or else I'm not going to make it. I know for sure I am not going to make it, this is too much. I need some sign from you. I just need one sign you will be with me. If I have to lose everything, then I need to know you will never leave me. I have lost my connection to my mother, my older brother is gone and now I'm going to lose my church family. I have been a mother to Peter since I was seven. And taking care of him, while being there for my mother, is more than I can handle. Please show me you'll be there."

I waited a little while. I don't know exactly what I was waiting for, but I knew there was going to have to be some type of physical evidence in order for me to be assured I wasn't going to face this alone. At that moment a gentle hand was placed on my shoulder. I thought it was Pastor J, but when I looked he was praying with another girl. Maybe it was one of the guys from my youth group. When I turned my head to see who was praying for me, I couldn't see much because the guy was so tall. Right away, I knew this was the same young man who caught my eye when I entered the gym.

He didn't say anything to me at the altar, he just kept his eyes closed and prayed silently. All of a sudden I heard the Lord say to me, "This hand represents the promise that I will never leave you or forsake you. I will always have my hand on your shoulder letting you know I am here. I will walk this painful journey with you and you will never be alone. You will be made whole again."

After that, I felt all the burdens on my shoulders lift. I felt the bag I had been carrying was not there anymore. I was ready to let it finally go and give it to God. I began weeping and all the young man did was squeeze my shoulder to indicate he was there, again not saying anything directly to me.

I stayed at the altar a while and the young man stayed with me the whole time, again, not saying one word to me. A friend of mine came over, but before I could say anything to the young man, he took his hand off my shoulder and was gone. I went to the bathroom to clean up and when I came out he was walking away with the same young lady who had ministered to me on the dock.

She looked back and saw me, then came over and gave me a big hug. We exchanged numbers and promised each other we would stay in touch. I wanted to thank the young man for praying with me. It was perfect, I didn't need a word spoken over me, I just needed that hand. But he was already walking off with a group of his friends. To go up to him now would seem weird.

THE HOME FRONT

When I went home, no one knew what had happened except me and God. Pastor J and Sister Claire prayed earnestly with me in hopes my mother would change her mind about leaving. I can't tell you the details, because I myself do not know them entirely, but those prayers worked because we never left for Florida.

God had plans for my mother, and slowly He was going to show her now that she was saved. She needed to learn about trusting Him. One day, grief and fear suddenly overwhelmed her. Her emotions began to run wild as she began thinking of how she was going provide for her family without my dad. She made her choice to stay here in NY with barely any family to support her. She sat at the edge of the bed and wept. Then, just as suddenly, she heard the audible voice say to her, "I will never leave you or forsake you." The voice, she told me, was so real that my mother stopped everything. Her tears stopped immediately because she was curious about this voice.

"I will never leave you or forsake you." Those words brought life back to her. She knew it was God and that she could trust in Him. That was the first, and the last time, that God ever spoke out loud to her.

She needed to trust in Him. To believe He was going to provide for her and be everything she needed. I saw God heal my mother slowly. She started to devote herself to God and church more. She was constantly reading her Bible and playing Christian music. I battled a bit with anger for a little while because I wished she had gotten saved earlier. If she had, I would not have had to go through what I went through.

I would find out later why it was the way it was. For now, God was in control and He allowed it at this time for a reason.

My mother needed God to come through because we were still struggling, and we didn't have a lot of food to eat. She couldn't work anymore than she already was, but her pay did not meet all of our needs. She had to sell my father's van that they had purchased, with hopes to get some money to continue paying off the funeral home.

I was getting ready for an event my youth group was holding one day when I saw my mother was worried about something. I asked her what was wrong. She said there was no more money and we had no food at all. She did not know how we were going to eat between Saturday and Wednesday, Wednesday was when she would get paid and would be able to buy groceries.

I was a little taken aback because I had not noticed how low we were on food. I heard the doorbell ring and put on my coat.

"Mom, you need to have faith. God will provide for us," I said to her as I rushed out the door.

My mom didn't know what to say. When I was older, she told me that I had so much faith that day, that it took her back at how I was not concerned at all. I went to church and had a wonderful time as usual. I never thought twice about the food at home. Usually I would have worried, but I believed what I said, I just didn't know how it was going to happen.

When I returned home hours later, I was blown away by what I saw. My mother was in the kitchen organizing boxes of food on the floor. The cabinets and fridge were bursting at the seams with food.

"What happened? Where did we get all this food?" I said.

"You were right, God did provide," she replied.

Apparently, God had put it in a neighbor's heart to take my mother to a wholesale place to buy whatever she wanted. This was the God I was serving. This was the last day we ever had a problem with food.

I knew for sure God was doing something in my mom when she called me to play Scrabble with her. I went to put on the Boyz II Men song like always. She told me to put on some Christian music after we had let the song play once. Yes, there were still tears because no matter how happy she was, she was still mourning, but her tears were a little different. She was saying good-bye to my father and saying hello to her new companion. I remember it well because it was also around this time the smell of death finally left and faded from our home. We felt like life was getting normal again.

Even though we had God, it didn't mean we had no struggles. It just meant when life got impossible, we had a Savior who would not leave us alone to fend for ourselves. With my father gone, I needed to take up more responsibilities at home and with Peter .

I ran a lot of errands for my mom, cleaned the house, was in charge of helping Peter with his homework, along with working on the weekends at one of my mom's clinics – and let's not forget I had to keep up my own homework as well. The trials of life started taking a toll on my body. I worshipped God and went to church every week, but I was still dealing with allot. I found myself constantly getting sick.

I was having problems keeping my food down and I was also having digestion problems. My mother brought me to the doctor because I was barely gaining any weight and it was getting worse. I had symptoms of a stomach virus with no relief for months. I was constantly vomiting and had diarrhea.

One night, I was on my way to the bathroom when something happened. It was late into the night and I was watching TV with my mother and brother when suddenly chest pains started coming on me. I could not find any comfort in any position I was in. The pain increased and increased till it hurt to take a breath. I got up and I started laboring in my breathing. My mother started to worry. I turned to walk back to her bed when she asked if she should call the ambulance. Before I could answer, I stopped breathing. I could not even gasp for air. It was like someone had their hands around my neck. I started clawing at my mother's clothes because I couldn't breathe at all. My mother started screaming for Peter to call 911.

My mother grabbed me and as I looked at her, the look of terror on her face made me feel helpless. Just when I thought I was going to pass out, my mother screamed out, "JESUS!!!" – air filled my lungs at once, and I dropped onto the bed. My first and only thought right at that moment was of my mother and how she could not handle another loss. I found it ironic that a few months before, I was trying to end my life; but now I was fighting for it.

I was rushed to the emergency room where they told me I had an extreme case of gastroenteritis. I was severely dehydrated and burning up with a fever of 104 and I didn't know it. My mother and my brother stayed in the emergency room all night while I received bags and bags of IV.

The result was that I was dealing with too much stress. In truth, there were times when I was so weak I couldn't move. I had missed many days of school because of it. One time, I started getting sick on my way to school. I tried to keep going, but I couldn't. One of my teachers asked if I was okay, but I was so embarrassed. I didn't want to tell her I was sick. After she left, I fell on the floor and almost passed out because I was in so much pain. I ended up leaving school without permission because I didn't want anyone to know what was wrong. I got very behind in my school work but always made just enough in my grades to pass. But no matter how sick I was, I refused to miss church. I found myself sick at times in youth group feeling like I was going to pass out.

After many months of testing, I was diagnosed with a chronic illness the doctors said could not be cured. They told us the condition would flare up in times of extreme stress and that I needed to change my eating habits. I left the part-time job over the weekends. Those steps helped greatly and my stress factor lowered.

By now a year had went by. Pastor J was my favorite person on earth. He took his role in my life seriously and I appreciated it. He called me every Friday to make sure I was coming to church and he would take the time to talk with my mother to see how I was doing in school. At 15 years old, I started liking boys. And Pastor J asked me about every last one of them. He teased me, but he also protected me from making stupid mistakes. Even if it was a boy from our own youth group, he made sure to be that father figure. It was the best feeling, to feel loved and cared for.

As Pastor J played the physical role of a father, my ability to bare my soul to God at the altar came easier. I cannot stress enough the fact that I spent a lot of time at the altar. Every Sunday and Friday when I attended church, I cried and wept and allowed the presence of God to break me. Most of the time I was praying for healing from this illness, but other times I was asking God to help me see myself the way He saw me. Every time I took that step to the altar, God met me without fail.

I didn't just wait to go to church and be in his presence, I regularly had times of worship at home as well. James had drilled it into my head that I could have the same God experiences at home as I had in church. I made sure to take a few days out of the week to be with God in my bedroom and just worship. The battle still remained with my insecurity, low self-esteem, and wondering when everything would just go away so I wouldn't have to feel the pain anymore.

It reminds me of a story my mother told me when she was a child. Due to a very bad fall, my mother had broken her shoulder. My mother was very poor as a child and was unable to afford medical attention, so her grandmother did the best she could set it back in place. Since she never got the right medical attention, it began to heal, but in the wrong way. She found it very hard from that point on to sleep or lift up her arm without feeling some sort of pain. Many years later, she went to a doctor and told him about the pain in her shoulder. He told her the only way to fix the problem was to re-break the bone and set it the right way so it could heal properly. My mom felt the pain of breaking the bone again was far worse than living with the current pain, so she decided it was best to just leave it alone. Besides, she had already grown accustomed to it by now anyway. To live with her current pain made more sense to her than breaking her shoulder all over again so she could eventually live with no pain. But what my mom didn't consider was, as she got older, the pain would increase and there would be a chance of arthritis in that same shoulder.

I was broken and found comfort in pornography, fighting and many other things. I was always in pain, like my mother, and I had my limits as she did. Confronted with some choices that needed to be made, I had to realize I was never going to be whole again unless I allowed God to address my deep rooted pains. I was scared if those things were stirred up

195

again I wouldn't be able to face them. Like my mom, I did not allow the great Physician to heal me, so the wounds of my past had to heal on their own and they would occasionally sting me. The idea of allowing God to "re-break" them scared me. Yes, I was saved and loved Jesus, but I have said it time and time again I was broken, wounded and hurt. If you think getting saved is the one and only step, I am here to tell you the truth, it's not. "Come as you are" doesn't mean He leaves you as you are. He wants you to come as you are so He can fix you.

"Being confident of this, that he who began a good work in you will carry it on to completion until the day of Christ Jesus." Philippians 1:6 (NIV)

I needed to make the choice to allow God to begin this painful process. I was not sure if I wanted to go through that again, but I had to choose. Was it better to stay with my familiar pain or would it be more beneficial to confront the hurts of my past in order to heal the right way? Could I risk the pain getting worse as I got older?

Chapter 12

THE MIND OF A TEEN GIRL

y relationship with God continued to grow slowly, while at the same time teenage life and all its pressures began to challenge me. My school was one of the largest schools in the area with an attendance of close to 2,000 students. In my sophomore year I realized more and more that holding on to my Christian views and values was harder than I expected. The teens around me were having sex, smoking, drinking and partying. It wasn't long before I was labeled as the "Good Girl" because I wouldn't involve myself with any of the nonsense in school. I know what you're thinking, and yes, you're right. This was a title totally opposite the one with which I was usually associated. I was completely different than what I had been before. I stayed to myself, and I tried my best to stay out of trouble.

I never had more than one close friend in school at a time because I came to learn too many friends meant a higher risk of drama. It was in Junior High (Middle School) I realized this lesson. I had a friend named Jennifer – and I still had the reputation for fighting. Jennifer came to me one day telling me about an argument she had with another girl. She wanted **ME** to help teach that girl a lesson. Had she made this request of me a year before, I might have helped her. This was around the time I was trying, with little success, to change my way of handling confrontations. Apparently, Jennifer wanted me to help corner the girl after school so she could stab her. I had already lived a life of violence. I wanted to be done with that. I didn't want that life anymore, so I told her "no" and asked her not to do it either. I was young, but I realized something that day. Jennifer had always been a really sweet girl growing up which is why this request from her was so shocking. It showed me that if she could be filled with so much hate, that she would want to go as far as stabbing a girl, then I couldn't continue to walk the way I had. I could not do it even a little bit longer; it could end up costing me my life, if not someone else's. That experience stuck with me and made me want to be different in High School.

CAN YOU SAY "OHH BOY!!!"

So here I was, fifteen and developing into a little woman. While I was learning how to see God more in the role of a father, I also found myself wanting a boyfriend. I was catching the attention of boys every day.

One day, I met a much older boy named Carl. I made him think I was older. Carl wasn't saved. I knew that, but I really didn't care. No one knew about him, not Pastor J, my mom, not even Peter. It began with him and I talking to each other, and then it grew into flirting. He eventually asked me out on a date. Fear gripped me because I couldn't tell him I was only fifteen and my "mommy" wouldn't let me out. So I thought up another solution that involved me sneaking out of the house without my mother knowing.

Carl was in his twenties, with a decent paying job and his own car. I was a little nervous about getting in his car to go on this date. We didn't go anywhere special, it was just a time for us to get to know each other better. We talked and shared about surface things. I told him about my father's passing, and I told him about my love for church. Even though the conversation was going well, I couldn't enjoy myself. I was so scared of seeing someone I knew walk into the place where we were eating. I was scared to have them call me out on my lie, and even worse tell my mom.

Our date was extremely simple. I refused to let him pay for me, it was a pride thing. Carl made it very clear that the next time we went out he would pay for everything, and that we would go somewhere more romantic. I really liked Carl, but the thought of having to lie to my mother again, and to him, was a little nerve racking. I knew I wasn't doing the right thing because I was hiding this from my mother and from Pastor J. I also knew if my father was alive the idea of me doing anything like this would have been an absolute joke. I was taking advantage of my mom and it was completely wrong.

After the date, he gave me my first real kiss. I was taken aback. I had to wonder what I was doing. This guy wasn't even a Christian, and I was getting involved with him. Stupid me decided to take everything I felt was wrong and push it all away. I didn't want to think about the negatives, let alone deal with them. I thought, "This was no big deal and what harm could it bring." I went upstairs and got myself ready for bed. I could tell God was not pleased. It was that awkward feeling of "I know you're there, but I'm going to pretend you're not," kind of thing. I felt His presence and I tried hard to avoid Him, but how can you avoid God?

"You know you can't keep this going."

"Why not," I replied bitterly.

I knew very well "Why not," but I just didn't want to hear it. I wanted someone to love me like all the other girls my age. They were in relationships, and that's what I wanted. It was my loyalty to God that was keeping me back from being the person I knew I could be. I was growing weary in well-doing.

I went into the bathroom to take a shower and slammed the door, as if that would keep Him out (I'm laughing at this now). He did not have to scream through a door or wait until I was done to face Him and continue the conversation. Nope,

He went right into the bathroom with me to finish what He started.

"What is it about him you like?" He asked.

"He makes me feel good about myself. He makes me feel that he would take care of me and love me. He makes me forget everything I have to deal with here. I'm a different person with him."

"I need you to end this as soon as possible. This is not going to end well. I have someone for you and I promise you he will be everything you need. Carl will lead you away from me, and I have plans for you."

"Fine!! I can't believe you're making me do this. Other girls are in relationships, why not me?" I said with tears in my eyes.

"Because you belong to me," He said lovingly. "And I have a plan, and a man for you."

I was so angry and frustrated, but more so with myself. I knew I was completely wrong and that this was a stupid idea from the beginning. How long could I keep up the lie anyway? It was best to end it before anyone got hurt.

I know to some this story sounds absolutely ridiculous, but that was, and still is, how God made sure to be a part of my life. I never ever treated Him like a guest in my life or as an acquaintance. I truly treated Him like my biological father, and in return, He treated me like His daughter. I was not serving the God my church created for me when I was young. I had gained a personal, intimate, and real relationship with Him as my Lord.

I understood if I was in my own mess for 12 years, doing whatever I wanted, I needed to give God at least the same amount of time to work in me and make me new. It was not fair for me to rush perfection.

MY KING OF KINGS

I had an unforgettable encounter with God on Christmas of 1994. My mother was watching a very old movie called, *The King of Kings*. It was a movie depicting the life and crucifixion of Jesus Christ. I have seen these kinds of movies in part before, but this time it was different. The movie had a bunch of close-ups of the man who played Jesus. As I watched the movie, I suddenly felt he was looking straight at me, right into my soul. I was drawn to this man on the screen, and I came face to face with the true understanding that Christ was tortured for me. The movie in no way showed the real experiences of what Christ went through, but the concept of what He did became real to me.

Please do not misinterpret what I am saying here. One of the reasons I try to maintain such an intimate relationship with God is because I truly see His sacrifice on the cross as an act of love for me. I believe I was on His mind when He walked on the earth. I believe that, even though it was 2000 years ago or so when He died. Christ loved me then just as much as He loves me now. I read the Scriptures by placing my name in them, because God had me in mind when He was writing them. I don't have to question the promises found in them. If God's Word says I am the head and not the tail, I believe He was talking to me, even though it was Moses writing it down. I don't question when He speaks, like others do, wondering if I imagined it or if it was really Him.

At the time I watched that movie, I already understood Jesus made a way for me to have a new life. It was what I was searching and striving for. What I didn't realize, until then, was there was more to Him than just a new life. I understood that He cared for me, and that His death was an ultimate price of His love. All this I learned in church. What I did not learn, was the extent of His death. I was not present to see my father die, so I didn't understand the horror of death. On top of that, Jesus didn't just die, He was put to death. And according to Scripture, He gave Himself up willingly. I understand that now, God allowed Him to be tortured for me. He was beaten, bruised, whipped, spat on, kicked, mocked, had His beard yanked out, endured the pain of a crown of thorns placed on His head and was nailed to a cross, just for me.

So that you don't think I am a heretic, let me be clear. I know Jesus died for all mankind, and that ALL who believe in Jesus Christ as their Lord and Savior are saved. At that moment of my "Revelation," if you will, I recognized He died for me. It became personal, not universal. And I don't think it is wrong of me to see it that way, even to this day. Even if no one else in all of time would have followed Him,

He still would have died the same way just for me. That's how I saw it that day, and that is how I continue to see it to this day. His love knows no limits. When I understand He had me on his mind, then I understand His act on the cross was a personal sacrifice, and I appreciate it so much more. I believe if you understand it that way also, His sacrifice may take on a greater meaning in your life as well. His title as SAVIOR will mean so much more for you.

So there I was. I started remembering every act of sin, sexual addiction, and pornography. I thought of every act of anger, rage, vulgarity, violence and rebellion. As well, I remembered every selfish thought of hopelessness, suicide, fear, pain, bitterness, insecurity and loneliness. He wasn't murdered, because willingly, He laid His life down. Christ was humiliated and stripped of everything for me. My mind flooded with understanding. Rather than living a life without me, He endured all this. Every single filthy act and word I ever did and spoke was placed on that cross. While on the cross, He **became ME**! He took upon Himself everything I was, every foul thing I ever said, saw and did. The burden of sin that fell upon His shoulders tortured Him more than the whips and nails ever could have. He **chose** to be separated from His Father so that I would never have to be.

As I watched this movie, I felt the presence of God fill my mother's room, but she did not feel what I was feeling. I soon could not hide my emotion as I watched my best friend being sacrificed on TV. I went into the living room, and all

I could do was sob. How could anyone love me so much he would go through all of that just for me? Is this the God I had been talking to this whole time? I felt like I was discovering who the God I served really was, all that I learned finally registered in my mind. The reality of Jesus' love humbled me right there where I was.

I put on worship music. I felt God tell me how much He loved me, even in my mess. It was like getting saved all over again. It was like the renewal of wedding vows. The act of doing so doesn't make you more married; it just means you now understand better what it is you've gotten yourself into. And yet, you're willing to do it all over again. I wept throughout the night. Every time I closed my eyes, the eyes of the man who played Jesus would appear in my head. The whole thing was amazing. At some point during the night, I had a vision of Christ, standing still just looking at me. His lips did not move, but I felt Him say . . .

"I am not on the cross anymore. I have risen. I defeated death, Hell and the grave. You are able to live a life free of the things that once plagued you."

As I continued following the Lord and seeking His face, I tried to live my life more for Him than for myself. I was completely free from my sexual addiction. Now I was set on being a witness for Christ. I felt the need to give back to God. My first step of faith was to break out of my walls of seclusion and to befriend people and try and help them. It didn't matter if they were from church or from school. I witnessed

205

to all my friends in school. Several of them came to church with me, and quite a few gave their hearts to the Lord.

I also lent myself to my friends in church; I tried to be there for them as much as I could. My mom got a little annoyed because my phone was ringing off the hook from the moment I came home till it was time to go to bed. I quickly gained favor with my peers, and they came to me with many of the harsh struggles they were going through. I was able to speak candidly about my own struggle and my own victories. It was through these moments of ministering to them that I knew God was calling me to more.

I also gained favor with my leaders as well, not just Pastor J. I was given opportunities to preach and teach a few Bible studies in youth group. The one preaching I remember most was a message on the disciple Peter. I loved the story of Peter because I felt I was just like him. He was getting praises from God one minute, and being told to get behind Him another. Peter was willing to step out of the boat and walk on water, but lost faith when the waves came in. He was willing to fight for God and cut off the ear of the soldier for the sake of Jesus' honor, but yet denied Christ three times out of fear of death.

In this simple Bible study with my peers, I shared the progression of Simon Peter. He was changing, but still making these historical mistakes. One day, Simon Peter received a revelation of who his mentor was. Jesus was not Elijah, or Moses, or even the recently beheaded John the Baptist. They were just a bunch of dead people compared to Jesus.

He knew Jesus was the Messiah, the Son of the Living God. After Peter declared who Jesus was, Jesus in return declared who Simon was.

"And I tell you that you are Peter, and on this rock I will build my church, and the gates of Hades will not overcome it." Matthew 16:18 (NIV)

Peter was told who he would be, but he did not change right away. He was still rebuked for trying to stand in the way of Jesus' plan to save the world. Simon Peter was told Satan wanted to sift him like wheat, and he was rebuked for living by the sword. Then later, he denied Christ three times in one day. Yet, in the time to come, Simon would help build the church and set in place the foundational doctrine by which we live today. Wow, talk about screwed up and confused. I would have been right there with him if I were alive at that time. I probably would have been Simon Peter's little sister.

The truth is this book is about a servant who was like this disciple. I know there are people out there with testimonies of falling and getting back up with, what seems like, very little effort. The truth is, not everyone's story is like that. My testimony is for those believers who fall 7 times but get back up 8 times. It's for those who didn't get it right the first time, or even the second.

My message on this dysfunctional disciple was more for me than for them. I needed to know for myself that even though my failures and victories were so close together, God could, and was, still willing to use me. I needed to know that eventually I would have more victories than failures. I also needed to know that in time, I would become every-thing God saw me to be, even if I didn't see it in myself. My focus needed to stay on the end result, that one day I would become a force not even the gates of Hell could stand against. I wanted to break down the walls that Satan thought could hold me back, and I wanted to go rescue the souls of those people who were hurting as I once was. I wanted to be a weapon for the Lord forged by the fire of life.

It was shortly after my new found desire that I felt God was telling me to be a youth pastor. Pastor J was not the perfect youth leader, and even though he made me angry at times, I loved him more than he knows. He never fully understood me and my passion, but he mentored me through my journey with God. He was there for me as much as he could be. His wife, Sister Claire, told me once that if he had a choice of a daughter, he would have chosen me. Many of the youth questioned if I had a crush on him, but that was far from the truth. He was my dad in many ways, and was the vessel God used to push me towards the Lord. I wanted to be there for others as he had been there for me. This was why I hung on his every word and stayed close to him. Under him, I learned more about the power of love and about the honor of teaching it to someone else.

Pastor J thought I would be a really good youth pastor's wife, but not really a youth pastor. He didn't think churches were going to accept female pastors. He was right, but I had a God in heaven who did not see as man sees. I was dead set against settling for being just the WIFE of a youth pastor. I loved Claire, but I didn't want to be home with the kids while my husband did all the ministering. As much as I loved my senior pastor's wife as well, she wasn't an example to me of a wife in ministry either. I wanted to be there with the youth, loving them and making a difference in their lives. I wanted to be active in their lives, helping to point them to God and giving back to them what was given to me. Being a wife who sat back and watched my husband do all the work was out of the question.

"THANK YOU"

Drama became one of the ways in which God began using me to minister. My home church was affiliated with a Christian organization that held a contest each year for all the youth groups in which they competed in multiple forms of talent. I decided to enter in the Drama Solo category, and I even wrote up my own script. When the day of the competition arrived, I became really nervous. I was in the audience as I waited for my name to be called. I decided to go out into the hall with one of my friends to get my nerves under control.

When I looked down along the hallway, two guys were walking towards me. I noticed right away that one of them was the guy who prayed for me at the retreat over a year ago. He was totally oblivious as to whom I was, but he stopped when he noticed I was nervous. He asked me if I was okay. I explained to him, without really looking at him, that I was nervous about my skit. He encouraged me about the skit and told me to breathe really slowly. He said everything was going to be okay. I said, "thank you," and he went inside to take his seat.

When my name was called, I went up and performed my skit. I did well enough to move on to the next level of the competition held in upstate New York at the next youth convention. When the competition was done, I had hoped to find the guy from before to talk to him. Unfortunately, it was really late and my group had a long drive home. As I walked outside, there he was talking to some of his friends. He noticed me, but we had to hurry up and leave. I didn't know when I would see him again, but I promised myself the next time I saw him I would make sure to talk to him. I don't know why I was so determined, but I needed to do this.

A month went by and an event was set up in the Bronx that gave me a chance to see him again. When we got there I looked around to see if he was there, but I couldn't find him. He was pretty tall and stuck out from most of the other teens. I figured I would have seen him immediately. Worship had ended, and the main part of the service was about to begin. As everyone was heading back to their seats, I saw him. He was at the far left side of the sanctuary. I wondered if I was actually going to get the chance to speak to him. As the service went on, I started feeling dumb, really dumb. Why was I making such a big deal about this?

Once the service was over, Pastor J gave everyone 5-10 minutes to go to the bathroom before loading up into the van to drive back home. He also wasn't too fond of the teens from the other groups. He felt many of them were disrespectful and rude. At other functions, they would behave in ways he didn't appreciate. We would go to the events, but very rarely did we stick around to mingle with the other kids. The other reason was because he always found the girls from our youth group exchanging numbers with the guys from other groups. He didn't like us losing focus when it came to the purpose of these trips and rallies.

As I walked outside, I looked around. There he was talking to someone, so I did it. I waited patiently, but then realized my time was almost up. So I nicely interrupted and asked if I could talk to him.

"Excuse me," I said, scared out of my mind.

"Hi."

When he turned around and looked at me, I realized how tall he really was, especially since I was quite a small thing compared to him.

"Do you remember me?"

He looked at me funny and said, "Aren't you the girl who was nervous last month at the competition? You won right?"

I felt so stupid, "Ah yeah, but I don't know if you remember praying for me at the retreat a year and a half ago? I was at the altar and you came up and stood behind me and prayed."

He looked at me weird and took a little while to think. You could tell he was trying to jog his memory. I was going to die right there if he didn't remember me.

"Yes! I do remember you. You were crying at the altar right?"

I let out a huge sigh of relief, which was great because I didn't realize until then I had been holding my breath.

"Yes. I needed to tell you thank you. I was going through a lot that day and I needed God to show me He was going to be there for me. That very small act of placing your hand on my shoulder did miracles for me. It just gave me what I needed to trust God."

I didn't want to tell him my dad had died and I was going to commit suicide before he prayed for me.

"You're welcome," he said seeming shocked and speechless.

After saying this to him, I pretty much had nothing left. I really didn't plan for anything more to say. Before I could even tell him my name, my friend called me and told me Pastor J was waiting and I needed to get into the van now. I told him goodbye and went into the van. As I sat in the van, that is when I realized I had not told him my name, and worse I didn't get his.

I continued to go to youth group. I felt God's calling on my life to minister to people more and more. The feeling of youth ministry was overwhelmingly strong. I started talking to Pastor J about it, and he recommended I attend the Bible School he graduated from, Zion Bible Institute. I wasn't too sure if I was ready for that. For many years I had hoped to be a doctor, and that's what I had geared my studies toward. My mother even connected me with a pediatrician in her office who became a mentor to me in the field. The doctor took such pride in my desire for this career pursuit. My aunt, Aaron and Matthew's mom, was equally proud of my pursuit. She told me that she would pay for the expenses of school if I continued towards that goal. Was I willing to put that aside to pursue a life of ministry? One thing I knew for sure, this was not going to go well with my mother. I didn't think she was ready for my decision, so I waited to tell her.

YOUTH CONVENTION (again)

It was April of that year and my youth group went to the youth convention located in Syracuse. This would also be the place I would compete in the next level of the competition. The day of the competition, I sat down waiting for my name to be called and I began to have a mild anxiety attack (WHAT WAS WRONG WITH ME?). What was really happening was I felt the skit I was about to minister was going to touch someone in the room. A heaviness for this unknown person was so great all I could do was cry. Wouldn't you know it, out of all the people in New York State, the same young man who prayed for me and who I saw months ago, came over to me.

"Hey." He couldn't call me by name because I had yet to tell him.

"Hi." I said totally embarrassed.

I felt like such a loser because each time he'd seen me I was a wreck. I know I appeared to be this overly emotional and super-spiritual girl.

"What's wrong?" he knelt down to ask.

I felt so stupid for saying what I was feeling, but I told him anyway.

"I feel God wants this skit to minister to someone and that it's not really for the contest. I'm just so nervous."

"Well then you have to do it girl. You got this. Don't cry. It will all work out."

He patted my leg, hugged me and left. He was so positive, but I'm sure he thought, "Something is wrong with that girl."

I was called up. I did my best, but I wound up crying though most of it. My youth pastor was there waiting for me at the edge of the stage with a big hug. He told me how well I did and made me feel great even though I felt like I bombed it. I wouldn't find out the results until the next day. My youth group left to go to the pool at the hotel in which we were staying. The rest of the competition wasn't finished yet. I left without telling my new friend my name . . . again! Maybe I'll see him walking around the conference.

That night was service, and like last year, God spoke to me, but this time He spoke about me being called into the Mission Field. It confirmed for me that Zion was the way to go. I knew it was time to talk to my mother. Unfortunately, I didn't see that young man at convention again. Maybe I would see him next year.

Chapter 13

LORD, YOU KNOW ALL THINGS

fter coming back from the convention, I waited for the right time to talk to my mother about going to Bible school. A few months passed before I decided to tell her about leaving the idea of medical school behind. I made sure to wait until she was relaxed in her room. Then explained to her what had happened to me at the convention. My mother was not having it. She was not in agreement at all with me going away to Bible school. My mom had given her heart to the Lord, but the idea of throwing away my plans to become a doctor, and instead to become a youth pastor, was simply ludicrous.

I found out when I was much older why my decision to go away for school was not a good idea in my mother's mind. The simple reason was she needed me. I had landed a summer internship at a Japanese bank in the city. It was paying almost

$1000 every two weeks and it helped my mother tremendously. If I pursued this, I could have been set financially at such a young age. I could stay home and work to help her with bills. Also, staying home meant I could help her with Peter, but I couldn't do it anymore. I was tired of being the one she dumped him on. I was now 16 years old and sharing a room with my 9 year old brother.

I was forced to take him everywhere. If I went out with my friends, he had to be with me. When I went to youth group, she would ask me to bring him at times. It went from taking him once in a while because she wasn't home from work yet, to taking him even if she was home. If I went downstairs to talk with a friend, he was there. When I was on the phone, he was there. Pastor J even started getting frustrated with my mother because we would go to events that were planned only for teens, and each time I would have to bring Peter along. When my father was alive, he would at least take Peter along with him on his van runs. He also wouldn't allow us to bother my mom when she came home from work. But she was here now, and she didn't know how to relate to him.

My responsibilities also extended to having to clean up after him. It did not matter if he was the one who made the mess. I was responsible for making sure he cleaned it up, and if it wasn't done right, I had to do it. I kept my room a mess, but the rest of the house I cleaned. Along with doing my own homework, I had to help him with his.

I quickly grew very resentful toward both of them. He didn't deserve my anger, but I had no one else to take it out on. I felt if life was different and I was given the role of his sister, and not his mother, then maybe my attitude towards him would be different. From the time he was born, I was taking care of him. I loved the moments we had together, but from the age of seven I was given this task of watching over him as if I was his parent. My mother expected too much of me and I was feeling it.

Mothering was so much more than going to work and coming home. It had been over a year since my father's death, and I was still waiting and wondering when my mother and I would be able to have a normal relationship with each other. When would she actually take time out for Peter and I? I loved the moments when he and I were there for her, but it would have been great if she would have asked me about my day and seem a tad bit interested in what was going on in my life.

I remember the day when I finally took out my frustration on Peter. It broke his heart. I had finally been given permission to have a friend come and sleep over. This was a treat. When my father was alive, the thought of having a friend come over was unheard of. I was excited to be able to have a girl with whom to talk and share. The only problem was that Peter was in the room with us.

He never spoke or did anything to us. He just sat in one spot with his Ninja Turtle action figures and played very quietly. He was behaving very well, not bothering anyone. What angered me was the fact that my mother was in her room, doing nothing. Why not call Peter in to watch a movie or do something with him? She knew I had a guest and that he was in the room, but the idea of spending time with him since I was occupied angered me more. I wasn't going to yell at her, so I yelled at him instead.

"Peter, why are you here?"

"I just wanted to be with you," he said very sheepishly.

"No, you can't be here. Go with mom!"

"But I want to be with you. I will be quiet," he said.

"No! You need to go away. You're always here and you never give me any space! JUST GO!!"

He was so hurt. With tears, he quickly gathered up all his toys and went into my mother's room crying. Within a minute my mom called me into her room.

"What happened?" she said.

"What do you mean?" When I looked, Peter was at the side of her bed hiding on the floor because he did not want me to see him crying.

"Mom, everywhere I go he's there. I have no time or space to myself. This is the first time I have a friend with me, and he's with us. I needed some space, so I told him to go."

"But you hurt him. He just wants to be with you. Look at him. He doesn't even want you to see him crying."

I felt bad. He was truly hurt and I knew it was my fault, but it just made me more resentful. I felt I needed to get out of the house as soon as possible. I was done being the one everyone leaned on while I had no one to return the favor.

This was the beginning stage of my mother and I butting heads. I'm not sure if this is the time all mothers start to have problems with their teenage girls, but I know we had a textbook relationship of love and hate. We were very loving one minute, and then we would be having arguments the next. I wouldn't say I started picking fights with my mom, but I was slowly losing respect for her as the days passed.

One day, we had a conversation about forgiveness because someone had done something horrible to her. I totally understood her hurt and frustration, but I told her forgiveness was the best way to handle the situation. My mom felt justified in holding a grudge against this person. Out of nowhere, I asked her if she thought I was justified for not forgiving my father or Matthew for what they did to me. She was puzzled by my question because she was aware of my father's cruelty, but not the full extent of it.

Not being sensitive at all about her hurt and love for my father, I began to dump on her what had been building up inside me for years. This was definitely not the time for this, but I didn't understand that. For the first time, I thought we had connected emotionally. I thought I could finally express to her all the horrors I experienced with my father. I tried to tell her what he said and did to me. I didn't get to say much. She was confused. In anger, she yelled at me and said she didn't want to hear another word from me. My actions that day caused more conflict and strife in my relationship with her.

NATALIE

I had applied and was accepted to Zion Bible College. Now it was just a matter of finishing off my senior year strong. God had done some amazing work in me that year. I was with one of my best friends named Natalie. We had known each other for many years. We went to the same elementary school, junior high school and now high school.

She wasn't saved when I met her but she was one friend I was able to convince to attend church with me. One warm Friday afternoon, after school, we didn't want to go home to wait for Pastor J to pick us up. We decided to sit on the benches at a pond nearby and talk for awhile. From there, we figured we could walk to the church when it was time for youth. The church was still a distance away, but we figured it would be fun; it was something different to do.

Natalie and I loved being with each other. We laughed and joked about everything. The distance between the pond and the church seemed like a few blocks, because we had such a great time. Personally, on the side, I liked this idea because if I went home my mom might have told me to bring Peter along to youth group. This way, there was no opening for her to ask me. Instead, I could be alone with my friends in peace.

As we sat by the pond, we noticed a group of girls and a guy coming. We decided it was time to go. If you grow up in the city, you learn this at a young age. When you see a large number of people, you go the opposite way. It may be nothing at times, but you don't take chances. The head of the group started to make comments about Natalie. It was clear they were here for trouble.

Man, I had not had a fight in a couple of years now. I was wondering to myself, "Was this going to happen now?" I told Natalie to keep going, but instead she wanted to mouth off to the ones who said something about her. I looked at Natalie. I was very determined to get out of there.

"It is time to go," I said.

As we were walking away, they continued to antagonize us. I searched for that rage that once fueled me for all those years before. I had to be ready if this went against us. I found nothing that would give me the strength to turn and confront these stupid kids. Natalie walked in front of me, and I walked behind her, pushing her so that she kept walking. Natalie continued mouthing off to them, but I told her to keep going.

Suddenly, I heard the Lord tell me to stop and turn around. One of the girls had a 2x4 and was going to swing it at my head. I stood looking her straight in the eye with absolutely no fear whatsoever. She paused and looked at me. And to my surprise, she put the 2x4 down and walked away.

I really didn't know if this is what would happen every time, but it was a great testament to me that God was with me at that moment. I didn't show any signs of being a coward. When I was younger, doing nothing meant I was that coward. If anything, I felt stronger than ever before. I knew I had the power to stand up for myself, but I chose to walk away instead. My time in High School was pure evidence I was not the same person any longer. I was not going to allow myself to take my issues and struggles into my own hands. I needed God to be the one to shine in me and nothing else.

MOLDING MY FUTURE

Shortly after, it was time to go upstate for convention again. It had been a whole year already. Natalie was able to come with me, and she loved it the moment we got there. She had never been to anything like this before. I knew we were going to have a wonderful time.

I was now 17 years old and months away from going to Zion. I applied even though my mom was against it. I wanted to receive one last confirmation from God, a final stamp of approval from Him that this was what He wanted from me. It was becoming more real that I was leaving everything, my church, my friends, my mother and my brother. Thoughts would come into my mind that maybe I was making a big mistake. The very first night of convention I went with an open heart waiting for God to speak to me. He did just that. God told me he had a totally new life for me, one that I could not imagine. He said if I would continue to trust Him, He would use me tremendously in ministry; and that He even had a family for me, but I needed to stay obedient to Him.

He confirmed to me that Zion was the place to which He was calling me. He would meet me there to show me what His plans were for me when I arrived. I became very emotional because I didn't feel worthy enough to be used. Even though I was saved, I still lived under the words of my past. The names I had been called by other kids and my father left lasting impressions upon me. It was hard to accept God's word over my feelings. I believed Him, but it was just hard to accept. No matter how unworthy I felt, I would continue to follow Him and see this thing through. I wanted to see what God could do with me.

The next day at the conference, Natalie and I decided we were going to walk around the hotel in which our group was staying. At the end of our walk, we started heading back to our room. I looked up and saw him – it was the guy from the other church who prayed with me over two years ago. He was in the hallway with a bunch of his friends.

I looked a little different than the way I used to look. I was not the tight shirt, short dress-wearing kind of girl trying to attract a lot of unwanted attention from guys anymore. I had adopted the style of dressing more like a boy. I wore baggy pants, long shirts and baseball caps. I was wearing exactly that when I saw him. I wanted to say something, but I didn't want to make a scene trying to remind him of who

I was in front of his friends. I headed past the elevators and tried to sneak past him.

"Hey, don't I know you?" he said.

He remembers me! "Yes," I said back.

We greeted each other and I introduced him to Natalie. We talked for a while as the rest of his youth group gathered in the hallway. His youth pastor, Mitchell, came in and started talking to the group about what they were going to do for the day. I wanted to leave, but the young man told me to stay. After Mitchell explained everything, he told everyone to join hands for prayer. I felt a little weird because Natalie and I were in the middle of all this. It was a very large group. Mitchell looked around to see who he could ask to pray, and surprisingly enough, he knew my name and asked me.

"Hey, how are you, could you pray?"

I was in shock, but prayed the best I could and then they all scattered. Mitchell came up to me and told me he remembered me from last year's competition. He was actually the youth representative for our area and hosted the competition that year. He was a great man, I felt blessed he remembered my skit.

Before I left, I showed the young man where my room was, which was around the corner from his. FINALLY I got the chance to find out a little more about him. I even got his name, it was Sam. He was a lot taller than I remembered him being last year. I thought he was in his early twenties, but he was seventeen years old just like me. By this time, some of the other girls from my youth group were trying to figure out who this was I was talking to all this time, so He introduced himself to them. They thought he was sweet. Our groups were on different schedules, but I knew if I wanted to talk with him now, he was just down the hall. Truth be told though, I was too scared to even approach him.

Later that day, I was in my room with a bunch of girls and there was a knock on the door. It was Sam. He wanted to talk. We didn't let him in the room because that was against the convention rules, so all the girls went into the hallway instead. They did this on their own. I told them I was going to be in the hall talking to him, and when they saw him, they volunteered to all come out. Before I knew it, one of the girls from my room asked him to bring her to his youth group to meet some of his friends. To my shock, he left, but it was no big deal to me. I mean, I didn't care (Okay, maybe I did just a little).

Pastor J later heard I had met a guy from another church, but I didn't tell him who it was because he had the habit of playing the father role way too well and might embarrass me in front of the guy. The last morning of the convention, Pastor J. sat next to me during breakfast and asked me how the convention was for me. I told him it was perfect and I loved it. He asked me about the guy I had met from the other church. I didn't tell him right away because he was not too fond of the kids from that particular youth group. He was honest with me and told me he had seen a lot of the guys from the other churches and many of them were disrespectful and not worth my time.

"The only one who has ever been nice and respectful was this tall guy from the youth group sharing the same floor as us," he said.

I laughed and told him that was exactly the guy I met. Personally, I don't think he felt Sam was anything near the kind of person I would have considered, and that's why he said it. I was normally into the bad boys who had a little bit of a fire in them. Sam did not seem to have that in him. He truly appeared to be sweet and respectful, totally different from the other kids in his youth group.

As we were talking with him, Natalie came into the place I was eating and said Sam was looking for me. My heart started beating out of my chest. He was at the front desk in the lobby of the hotel. He wanted to talk with me because he was about to leave with his youth group to go to the last service, and there was no guarantee he would actually see me because there were so many people.

"I wanted to get your number so we wouldn't lose contact again," he told me.

I was so excited. I started searching frantically for a pen, but all I had to write with was my eyeliner pencil. He was a little surprised at my enthusiasm. We exchanged numbers and that was the last time we saw each other on that trip. This was my last convention before I went to Zion, so who knew when I would see him again.

The next day after getting home, I quickly started thinking that maybe I should call Sam. I didn't want to seem too eager, so I decided to call him next week instead. I went in my mom's room to watch TV when the phone rang. Peter came in.

"There's a guy on the phone for you," he said.

"Who is it?" I asked.

"He said his name is Sam."

I couldn't believe this, it couldn't be the same guy. I ran in the living room and grabbed the phone. It sure was the same guy!!! He wasted no time calling me. We had a great first phone call. We talked from 7:30 to 11:00 that night. We shared as much as we could. He was so easy to talk to and the conversation flowed so well.

He was a lovely young man, a little too good to be true. We established a very interesting friendship from the beginning. We spoke almost every day for hours. I started to grow attached to this new friend. Sam started making references about us getting into a relationship with each other, but the truth was I was going to Zion in four months. I didn't know what to do. I didn't think it was wise to even think about dating because I knew it was a recipe for heartache. Pastor J told me when he was in Zion, different people would meet at the school and then get married. He said they would jokingly call the school "Zion Bridal Institute" instead of Bible Institute because of the high rate of marriages amongst the students. I had some fears about getting involved with him because I was leaving to go to a school over 200 miles away soon. If what Pastor J said was true, I might fall for someone else in the school.

One day, Sam and I had our regular phone call. Everything was okay until he started talking about moving our relationship to another level. I told him I didn't want to. The biggest problem we faced was that he lived in the Bronx and I lived in Queens. For those who don't know, those are two totally different areas of New York City. A train ride from where I lived to where Sam lived was just about 2 hours. Driving time took about 45 minutes in good traffic (which was rare), and neither of us had a car. Added to that, was the fact that my mother would never let me go to see him regularly.

After telling him no, Sam left the topic alone and moved on to other things. It didn't scare him off. He told me it was fine and that he enjoyed our friendship. It showed me he was talking to me because of our friendship, and not because he sought something more.

I found myself thinking about him all the time, however. Eventually, I really wanted to meet up with him. I don't know why I was so taken aback by this guy, but I decided I was going to take a chance and date him. I didn't want to live with the regret of not trying. I lied to my mother and left school early (I know, not the best way to start a relationship). The neutral spot for us to meet was the city (Manhattan to non-New Yorkers)–where he worked after school. Natalie came with me, and a friend of his joined us also. We had a wonderful time.

I felt bad for sneaking around, but I wanted to see him. And I knew my mother would never let me go. I eventually told my mom I wanted to be in a relationship with him. Even though she didn't feel good about it, she gave me the okay. The distance that existed between us made it impossible for us to see each other on a regular basis. That did, however, help a bit with the fear we had about the longer distance that would exist once I left for school in Rhode Island.

We made the decision we were not going to complain about only having 3 months until I was gone, instead we were going to enjoy every moment. I grew to care for him dearly, and this just led to me questioning if Zion was the right choice. I was battling with the idea of leaving him. He showed me true love, and I didn't want to lose it, I couldn't lose it.

One day in early August, I met Sam again in the city to spend the day together. We had so much fun. We saw a movie, went window shopping and then went for a walk through Central Park and talked for hours. It was one of the best times I ever had. Sam started talking about us and our relationship as if there was a forever for us. The conversation made me feel uncomfortable and I wanted to end it quickly. He knew allot of my testimony, and that made him care for me more. It was clear he was in the relationship to take care of me and give me something I never had before, but I was set against it.

"I don't need anyone taking care of me. I can take care of myself," was what I told him.

I felt I was letting my guard down with this guy, and I didn't like it. I liked him, but I didn't like the way I was feeling with him. All my life I would shut people out – there were only a few people I trusted, and he had not earned that trust. I remembered what happened with Carl, and the last thing I needed was to put my heart into this new guy with his fake promises and big dreams. I had seen those stupid girly flicks where the girl has a knight in shining armor who treats her in way she had never been treated. He loves her, understands her, and then she falls for him and they live happily ever after. I just couldn't believe for that, it was too far- fetched.

Sam was always loving, patient and kind . . . what was he up too? I was going to be smarter than that. I wasn't foolish. This relationship would never work anyway; the odds were too great against us.

I had spoken to Pastor J about going away and being in a relationship with Sam at the same time. He suggested the best thing to do was to break it off. He continued to say our relationship stood a very slim chance of handling the long distance, and that very few ever did. I refused to become one of those girls who gave up everything for a guy because she was scared he would cheat on her or lose love for her. He felt I needed to think this over and do the right thing.

Pastor J was right–I did have to make a choice. I started crying and praying about everything. I wanted God to tell me what to do. He was so clear when I was getting involved with Carl, but He was not saying much now when it came to Sam. He was always so talkative, but now He chose to be silent. I told Sam I didn't think we were going to make it, and that maybe we should think about calling it off. He was very honest with me, and told me he had his reservations as well.

He had an ex-girlfriend whom he dated in High School for 3 1/2 years. She went away to college and their relationship did not last the distance between them. She hurt him tremendously, and the last thing he wanted was to go through that again. But for some reason, Sam was willing to try and see if we could make it work. I considered not going to Zion but Sam was totally against it. He wanted me to do exactly what God had told me to do before he came into my life.

This would be one of the hardest decisions in my life. When I first applied to Zion, I wasn't willing to even entertain the idea of staying home, but now things were different. God knew exactly what He was doing by instructing me to go to Zion first, before allowing me to build a relationship with someone. Had the situations happened in reverse order, I don't think I would have left. I know now why we missed all those opportunities to exchange numbers and why it took so long for me to even know his name. God knows for sure I would have gone against my word.

He had a plan for me, and I needed to continue to go after it. I needed to see if He was actually going to fulfill all these promises, so I had to do what He said.

Chapter 14

THE YEAR OF NEW BEGININGS

REMEMBER, THE CHOICES YOU MAKE ALSO AFFECT THOSE WHO LOVE YOU

As hard as it was for me to leave, it was a lot harder on someone else having to watch me leave. Peter had made it through my father's shooting and death, but what hurt him most was when I finally left to go to Zion. He told me, years later, how he viewed my leaving and the weeks leading up to it. We were all each other had. He understood me, and I understood him. My leaving left him feeling he had no one to turn to. When I would talk about finally getting away, he took it as me finally getting away from him. He thought I didn't want to be around him anymore. I did not realize how much I meant to him. In my quest for God, I didn't think about my brother at all. It never occurred to me to explain why I was leaving or to see what it was doing to him. I wanted out and I wanted change so badly, I didn't think about how this was breaking him.

I'm so sorry.

MY FIRST TIME AWAY FROM HOME

It was August of 1995, and it was the hardest decision I ever made. I was no longer leaving to get away, my purpose by this time was different. I was going to Zion with complete reservation, unsure where this road was going to end. My mother, Peter and Natalie came along as Pastor J drove me to Zion to help me settle in.

When the time came for me to say my good-byes to them, it all became real. This was the decision I had made. I was going to be alone. I was not living around the corner, I was 4 hours away with no one familiar in sight. I didn't want to show any fear or regret, but I couldn't help it, it was all there. As they drove away, I wanted to run after the van and tell them I made a mistake and wanted to go home, but I didn't. Instead, I went into my room and cried with my face in my pillow until I fell asleep.

The school was old fashioned in design. There were no phones in the rooms, and unlike today, cell phones were for those with serious money. There were about 9 or 10 pay phones everyone in the whole school shared. I searched frantically for the phone card Sam bought for me before I left. I went to the pay phone on my floor and called him. He picked up immediately. The sound of his voice filled me with so many emotions.

He asked me how I was doing, all I could say was I wanted to come home. I told him I had made a mistake and wanted to leave. I felt like I wasn't going to make it very long, and classes hadn't even started yet. He listened to me cry and told me he believed I could do it. He encouraged me to stick it out for as long as I could. If it still wasn't working out after some time, then maybe my mother would arrange for me to come back. I knew it was what God had wanted. He had called me here for a reason, but I just couldn't see it. It was my first of many lessons.

<u>Doing the will of God is not always easy</u>. If you look at some of the great men and women in the Bible, you'll see that each one went through great difficulty. Look at Moses, God wanted him to deliver the children of Israel, but he needed to first face Pharaoh. There was Abraham – he was called to be the father of many nations. He had to journey through unknown territory, and when his wife could not conceive, he had a son with another woman. Then there was David who was told he would be king. What he wasn't told, was that he had to run and try to stay alive because the current king would be out to kill him with every chance he had.

We think doing the Will of God is always easy and fun. Not all the time. Most of the time, we can be like Moses, questioning why God even picked us. Or maybe like Abraham, thinking that maybe God missed a couple of steps, so we try to help Him out and give birth to an "Ishmael" – the enemy of our promise. With David, the opportunities to take down Saul were present on a number of occasions. He could have proved his power by taking down the king and claiming the throne for himself, but David knew not to give in to his flesh.

"For the flesh desires what is contrary to the Spirit, and the Spirit what is contrary to the flesh. They are in conflict with each other, so that you are not to do whatever you want." Galatians 5:17 (NIV)

My flesh wanted nothing to do with the will of God, it wanted to do the total opposite. A few days went by and I felt God tell me to do something very hard.

"If you want Sam, you must let him go," He said

"What??" I thought. "I gave up Carl, now you want me to give up Sam? Am I never ever going to be with someone?"

"I didn't say break it off, I said you must let him go. This relationship will not last if you keep it in your hands. I want you to let him go and be willing to lose him for my sake. Take the whole school year and fast one day out of the week for my will to be done."

I did just that, again I trusted God. I still spoke to Sam on the phone and wrote him letters, but the idea of quitting and going home was out of the question. I needed to stay put and finish the fast so I could see what God had planned for me.

I guess Sam and I were blessed, because we had to learn early in our relationship the importance of putting God in the center of everything. I know many Christian couples who don't understand this. They place each other over God, and it always comes back around to bite them later. I knew that if I didn't do this, I was going to make decisions I would regret in the years to come.

I met a lot of people on campus, but I still felt alone. This was all new to me, I was never on my own like this before. It wasn't too long though, when I realized why God had brought me to Rhode Island (The school has since relocated to Boston). I was sitting in a chapel service, and the staff had carved out a time for students to come up and share testimonies.

I sat there listening to testimony after testimony of students talking about the goodness of God. I was encouraged by the stories they told of how God had called them and brought them to this point in their lives. Then a girl came up to the stage, she grabbed the microphone and started talking. She told us about her wonderful Christian family. Her father was a pastor and her mother was a stay at home mom. They weren't rich, but they were well off. She continued to explain that she had gone to church her whole life with her siblings and that everything was wonderful.

She then said to us she walked away from God at one point in her life because she basically had no struggles. Her life was so sheltered it suffocated her and she wanted out.

She was given God on a silver platter, but she was serving the God that her parents gave her, not the one she chose to follow. Then she made a statement that made me want to stand up and scream:

"I have heard of people who had been abused and molested, and I wanted that because I had no testimony. They seemed to be closer to God because of it."

I still get a little angry at that statement, even though I understand what she was trying to say. Back then, however, I thought she was nuts.

"What is she talking about?" I thought to myself. "She wants to be broken like I am?"

The young lady ended her "testimony" by saying she now understood she needed to serve God in a more personal way built on her own experiences.

I went to my room and had a moment of anger I had not had in quite some time. I almost ripped my room apart. I lit erally threw a tantrum. If my roommate had walked in at that moment I would have taken it out on her too. How could that girl say she wanted to be like me? She would want to give up her life with her loving parents to be beaten, cursed at, humiliated and abused as I was? Did she want to feel what I was feeling at that moment, broken, hurt, insecure, fearful, and empty? She had no idea what she was saying.

I cried because I didn't see back then anything in me that had worth. It was then I realized there was only one thing that gave me purpose . . . it was God. I loathed who I was, but I was in love with who I hoped to become in Christ. It made no sense, but yet, made all the sense in the world. Nothing within me was worth living for except for the God who took up residence in my heart.

Are you ready for this? It all happened in my moments of abuse and pain. I can tell you right now I had a real relationship with God, and it had been birthed through my times of desperation. I finally saw I was not like other people. I could not make one move without consulting Jesus. I would wonder why it was so easy for people to do things they knew were wrong and against God. I had lived that life, but now I was done with those things. I didn't want it anymore.

Those other people who would choose when they wanted to serve God, and when they wanted to live as the world would have them live, made no sense to me. I saw God as my lifeline. In my mind there were no other options. My life before was so destructive and suicidal, but now, I had everything to live for because I walked with my Savior. I knew each and every day I walked was a miracle because I should have been dead. Praise the Lord because nothing has changed since then.

That night I needed the embrace of God to comfort me. I began to worship and weep as I felt His presence swallow me up again. It was the strongest I had ever felt Him. That moment stayed with me for quite some time. It was at this season of my life God gave me a new scripture to hold on to:

"You intended to harm me, but God intended it for good to accomplish what is now being done, the saving of many lives." Genesis 50:20 (NIV)

I'm sure you can see how this verse inspired me in my situation. In a time of devotion, God spoke to me and explained the enemy had meant to destroy me. He continued to tell me about how He had a calling for me.

"I have a purpose for you. I am going to use you to save many lives. There are many who have gone through what you have gone through, and I am going to use you to set them free. You must be obedient and trust me."

Only God could take moments of pain and turn them into powerful tools He would use to save lives. Going to Zion was like going to an emotional, spiritual boot camp. I wanted more of God, and He did not disappoint. I not only grew in my knowledge of the Scriptures, but I also grew in my ways of devotion and prayer. I learned His voice more – and even better – I began to know His heartbeat.

The experiences I had were amazing and full of wonder. I would rush back to my dorm room after classes and put on worship music. Every chance I had I would spend in prayer and devotion. These moments in my room healed many of my old wounds. It was like God had given me a concentrated dose of love. That whole first year became a time of connection and study. Each experience I had with God slowly erased the stains from my past that had blackened my heart.

This became my routine for the remainder of the year, and I loved every bit of it.

FORGIVENESS

At one point during my times with God, He spoke to me about forgiving my father. It was going to be a hard thing to do, but I could not continue to walk in God's presence if I had un-forgiveness following me. This was not a part of my plans for the future at all. I couldn't bring myself to do it. How do I forgive a man that was dead? This whole thing set my mind back into a horrible place. I tried to come up with the words, but I just couldn't do it.

I needed to hear my dad say he was sorry for what he did to me. Then, at least, I would have compassion. That wasn't going to happen. When my dad died, he died in my mind as the man who beat me, and did so much more. There was no compassion for that man. God was teaching me about His love, and I realized that un-forgiveness was not an ingredient that mixed well with His. I needed to get rid of it in order to move forward.

"For if you forgive other people when they sin against you, your heavenly Father will also forgive you. But if you do not forgive others their sins, your Father will not forgive your sins." Matthew 6:14-15 (NIV)

The truth is, you can't become a Christian without first being forgiven. It is the first seed, so to speak, that God plants into us for us to be saved. I needed to be forgiven from the wretched things I did and would later do. I know that here, I'm pretty much being an open book, but in reality, I am a really private person. I still have my issues, and I am nowhere near perfection. The difference now is that I don't hide what I feel, and that helps me seek after His forgiveness every day. Back then, I kept most of my emotions towards people bottled up inside, and now God wanted me to let them out.

I acknowledged Christ forgave me, and for the most part, I felt I forgave the important people. I knew I had to let go of all my hurts, but man it was hard. God was asking me to forgive as He had forgiven. If I refused, how could I expect Him to forgive me of my sins? This was not easy. But now, my ongoing refusal to forgive my father became the latest sin I needed forgiveness for.

It was hard for me to receive the Matthew 6 scripture because I felt justified in my anger. Have you ever felt justified for keeping someone a prisoner in your mind because they wronged you? I sure did. I was a child, and my father was a grown man who knew better. In my mind, I felt the rules should be different for me.

God led me to the story found in Matthew 18 of "The Unmerciful Servant." My current Senior Pastor just happened to preach a message on this story a few weeks ago. My pastor knows this topic is a struggle for me even now.

He teases me every time he is going to teach or preach on it. Jokingly, I ask him to please move on to something else, but God continues to give him this subject to bring to the church regularly. I asked him for his notes so I could use some of his message. He told the story so well I wanted to put in his version.

"A servant owes the king a huge amount of money he'll never be able to pay back. Initially, in line with the world's way of thinking, the king orders that he, his wife and his children, along with all their possessions, be sold to recover part of the debt that's owed. Just about then, in a flash of desperation, the servant falls to his knees and begs for mercy. 'Be patient with me and I'll pay back everything I owe', which everyone knew was never going to happen.

But the surprising part of the story is that the king does in fact have mercy on the servant and not only vacates the sentence, he cancels the debt. This is far more than the man had asked for or could have even imagined or hoped. This is where the difficulty, the challenge and the cost of forgiveness become clear. In the world the rule is you owe, you pay and to underscore how seriously this rule is taken in the world, one commentator reminds us that the street name for someone who lends money is a loan SHARK – not a loan bunny or a loan poodle. In the world – you owe – you pay – or you're devoured. In this story Jesus uses to portray forgiveness as worship, the king turns this worldly rule on its head so that now it's <u>you</u> owe – <u>I'll</u> pay. You see, the fact the king was forgiving and cancelled the debt didn't mean the debt just went away, there was still a vast amount of money to be accounted for, and somebody had to absorb the loss of that money. In this case, it wasn't the person who owed the money, it was the one to whom it was owed. So yeah, forgiveness is a costly form of obedience, perhaps the most costly, but that's also why it's one of the highest forms of worship we can offer."

My pastor was so right, it's one of the highest forms of worship we can offer. In Zion, when I read this story, I knew I was the servant who could not pay back to Jesus all he had done for me. Even if I were to sell all my possessions to the poor and sell my soul to the highest bidder, I wouldn't even dent the debt I owed God. I was so grateful for His act of forgiveness, even though I knew it was given undeservingly.

For months, I would put on worship music and have my devotions with God. I didn't think anymore about forgiving my father and all those who violated me. I truly believed I was exempt, and that because of my circumstances, the Scripture did not apply to me. I did not think God could really expect me to forgive my molester. He took my innocence and my childhood. How could God want me to forgive my father who wanted to literally kill me? He hated me. I was so afraid of him I would randomly wet myself when he would speak to me. "Never," I thought to myself. "Never."

My pastor's message continued:

"After the king cancels the debt of the first servant, a debt he could never repay, that first servant goes out and encounters the second servant, who owes him a few dollars. Now you would think that first servant would still be basking somewhat in the afterglow of having just passed from death to life, which is what makes his behavior toward this second servant so shocking. He grabs the second servant and begins choking him. Then immediately, demands repayment of the debt the second servant owes him. When that servant begs for mercy, just as he had begged for mercy from the king, he refuses – and has the man thrown in prison until he can pay the debt. Of course all this news eventually makes it back to the king, who calls the first servant in. He declares him to be WICKED and UNGRATEFUL, and in his anger the king turns the man over to the jailers to be tortured <u>until he pays back all he owes,</u> which remember, would be impossible."

I remember my thoughts when I read this story back then.

"Jesus, do you really think what they did to me and what they owe me is that small, compared to what I did to you?"

It wasn't small to me. Then I thought of the times I rejected Jesus when I was younger, and when I did unthinkable things. I remembered my impure thoughts. Even though my cousin Matthew helped to put them there, I was still accountable. I thought about my desires to kill my father. According to God's word, with my thoughts, I murdered my father long before he died. I had realized the severity of Christ's act on the cross when I saw that movie almost two years ago, but now I was seeing it as the debt I could never repay.

It was time to do for others what God did for me. Not to sound like a broken record, but IT WAS HARD!!! Unlike the servant, I did not want to be considered wicked and ungrateful by my Master. The rest of the story ended with Jesus explaining how God would do the same:

"This is how my heavenly Father will treat each of you unless you forgive your brother from your heart." Matthew 18:35 (NIV)

Jesus was clear to say that our heavenly Father will treat us the same. I was afraid of losing what I had with God, so I started the process of forgiveness. I'd be a liar if I told you at that exact moment I forgave everyone for all they had done to me.

If you haven't caught on yet, forgiveness is the hardest subject for me to swallow. This is why I don't swing that sword into anyone's direction before swinging it in my own first. As I mentioned before, this was not the first time my pastor preached on forgiveness.

Once, he did a whole series on "Unconditional Forgiveness"–it was about 3 years ago. That was so hard for me to sit through, because at the time, there were so many people who were getting under my skin. I wanted to lose my patience, but I kept on listening to his messages on forgiveness. Every time he uttered the word, I lovingly wanted to slash his tires, or put salt in his coffee or even remove the screws from his chair in his office (Don't worry. We have a relationship like that. The stories I could tell of what he has done to me in return! Maybe one day in another book).

It was a topic that grounded on my soul, even though I was now in my thirties. True forgiveness is a process. It doesn't happen overnight, despite what anyone tells you. For this reason, Jesus said you need to forgive 70 x 7. The fact is you may think the issue is gone and dealt with, but then there it is, it just comes up again. Someone may not do something to you 490 times, but that may be the amount of times you think on it. Every time that event comes into your head, you must choose to forgive. I tackled the hardest one first and wrote my dad a letter.

Dear Dad,

I know this seems foolish of me to be doing this now, but I wanted to talk with you. I have been battling in my heart with what happened when you were here. For many years, I lived with pure hate towards you. You took my childhood from me. You treated me like I was trash. You never thought to love me or to talk to me. YOU NEVER HUGGED!! You NEVER LOVED ME.

I spent my life with you waiting for you to say those three words, "I love you," and I waited for nothing. You died, and you never ever said it to me. Instead, you beat me, slapped me, cursed at me, called me some of the worst names and you didn't think twice of how you broke me in half.

I loved it when you got stoned or drunk because that was the only time you were nice to me. All the other times you were the meanest man ever, but when you got drunk and high, you were so loving and caring to me. You treated me the way I was supposed to be treated. I don't know which one was the real you, or who was really talking. Maybe the drunk you was the real person who couldn't come out when you were sober.

I wanted to write you because after going through all this, I wanted to kill you. I even thought of stabbing you in your sleep or taking your security gun and shooting you. I felt that if God didn't want me to kill you, then maybe I would run away or kill myself, but there was a God in heaven who stopped me. I hated your guts. I mostly hated you for making me feel this way about you. A little girl shouldn't feel like this towards her father.

I'm writing you, because now I know you didn't know better. I know you were a hurting man and you only knew how to hurt. I am in the process of forgiving you, but I need you to forgive me too. I am so sorry for hating you. I am so sorry for wanting you dead. I don't know where you are, and I don't know if you are in hell. I may have put you there because I wanted you gone more than I wanted you saved. I know I can't take back what I prayed, and you can't take back what you said and did, but know that I am sorry and I need forgiveness just as much as you do.

I wish things could have been different. Despite it all, I will learn to love you.

Your Daughter

Not the best letter. I know. But it was all I could do at the time.

Again, I don't want to fool you into thinking this happened over night. I needed to place my father on the altar whenever I was in a new stage of life and the bitterness and resentment wanted to creep back. I needed to continue to give it to God and see His hand in my life. It took several years to be totally free, but this was the place I made my first step on the path of letting go.

Today, twenty one years later, I have a picture of my father at the side of my bed. He is in his security officer's uniform writing a parking ticket (I don't know who took a picture of that, but I have it now). There are times I randomly look at it and cry, because I know if he were alive today, with God anything would have been possible. I actually love him and my heart hurts not knowing where his soul lies. I have come a long way, but there is still plenty for God to do in me at thirty six.

ARE YOU REALLY READY?

As I continued to trust God, He would waste no time in dealing with the next issue at hand. Going to Zion, for me, had little to do with the classes. Sure I learned a great deal, but I feel I was not there for just that. God used that place as a safe haven for me to hear from Him better and develop our relationship. It was miles away from all family and friends, even Sam.

I started to ask God about my relationship with Sam. I was still fasting once a week but I needed to know what the future was for us, if there even was one. I was completely in love with him, and the thought that he may not be the one was ripping me apart. It's funny, because in our time of dating Sam had made one request.

"Never tell me God had told you that we are to be married," he said.

He felt that was just a trap, and he had heard too many girls say it to their boyfriends. So I knew if God was going to tell me I was to be his wife, it would have to be from Sam himself.

One day, he called me after a choir performance his youth group held. He was so emotional, and that was not like him. He was a very loving man, but he never got this emotional. He went on to explain that during one of the songs, the power of God just filled the place. Everyone, the singers, musicians and audience felt it. He began to cry as he sang because God started dealing with him.

"God showed me the two of us in ministry together. You and I were holding hands, but I didn't know it was you at first. We prayed for people, I heard worship music and I saw people in the distance coming to us to for help. It was so powerful and overwhelming with all those people around, but yet peaceful because God was there guiding me. Then I was able to look at whose hand I was holding, and it was you. You were experiencing all this with me and we were a team."

Was this really happening? Sam kept saying God was going to use us tremendously and that God would provide for us.

Now it was my turn, I needed to hear from God myself. Shortly after our conversation everyone was gathered in the chapel... I loved that place... and we were listening to a guest speaker. All of a sudden, everything went silent and I could hear nothing but the speaker on stage. It was like he looked right at me.

"Do you think you are ready for the calling God has for you?"

Then God took over and said, "You need to think about the role of being Sam's wife. It will not be easy. It takes a strong woman to hold him up."

I went into my room that night, my normal meeting place with God and He started showing me Sam had a great calling. He was going to minister to many young people and we were going to be a team in everything we did. He needed a strong wife, and if I was taking the position as his wife, I was also taking on his burden of ministry. I was to hold his arms up and help him through it all.

As I sat there, I was blown away by the calling and the responsibilities that came in the vision. I had to ask God something.

"I notice that other people have a certain place to which they feel called – Africa, China, India – but you haven't told me where we are going."

The Lord told me I would start off at my home church and from there it would spread. He said He had not shown me a certain place, because I am called to the whole world. How was I supposed to do that, I thought? I had plenty of questions, but God wasn't going to tell me everything. Besides, I am sure if He did give me the details of how He was going to use me, Sam and I would have started to doubt.

I needed to think about all this. Sam was not just the man I would marry, but his calling was great. With the issues God was confronting me with, I had to choose if this was the life I wanted to live. Being a wife is just as much a calling as any other position, and that is the same for being a husband. Nowadays we rush into marriage because of the emotion behind it, but the reality is emotions fade with every passing morning. You realize your spouse has bad breath in the morning, they have obnoxious eating habits and the bathroom doesn't smell so fresh after they leave it. Marriage is a calling, and that's what God intended it to be.

God showed me a portion of the life I was called to live, and He gave me the chance to decide if I wanted the job or not. I told Sam. It was like we could finally breathe. Before, it was like our hearts were preparing to be broken in case the distance became too hard for us to handle. Now, things were different, God had spoken to both of us. We started talking about marriage with real confidence.

THE LOSS OF HIS DAD

The summer of 1996 was quite interesting. Sam took me out on a date one day, and we had a wonderful time as usual. The night was warm so we decided to sit outside and talk. This was when I was able to get a more detailed story about his dad.

Sam was 12 years old when his father, Manuel , was murdered. It was just a couple of months before his birthday. Sam told me his father was a wonderful, loving man. He was an elder in their church, and he worked really hard to support his family. He wasn't perfect, but he did as best as he knew how by his family, and they all loved him. Sam is the youngest of three boys, so he didn't get to experience his dad's discipline as much as his older brothers did. His mother absolutely loved him, and the loss of her childhood sweetheart devastated her for many years.

No one could give his family the actual play by play of what happened, but according to the police on February of 1991, Sam's father went to the supermarket to pick up milk and found himself in the middle of a robbery. Manuel worked as a Supermarket Manager, and he was also a deli owner. He had been a victim of several robberies before. On some occasions, he would chase down the thieves and tackle them to the ground. He was also a Vietnam Veteran.

According to Sam, even though this wasn't his store, his dad most likely intervened out of pure instinct. There were women and children present, and the robbers were holding up the place at gun point. Sam's mom once said that Manny was not the kind of man to see something like this go down and just stand back and do nothing. The police believe he went to one of the robbers, grabbed him from behind and tried to wrestle the gun out of his hand. The robber was able to bend the gun behind his head and pull the trigger. The gun went off and shot Manny in the throat. After the gun went off, the thieves all left immediately and were on the run. Manuel died immediately.

The media covered the story. Manny's killer was on the loose, and they needed the community to help find him. Sam's extended family is pretty big. His cousins knew people in the streets, so they too began their own manhunt in the neighborhood. Ultimately the man turned himself in out of fear that the wrong person would find him.

Sam told me the story that August night, and it broke my heart. Then something clicked. As Sam spoke, I realized his dad was killed the year my father had gotten shot. At the summer camp I attended, if you remember, I was telling my father's story and somehow one of the camp counselors knew about what had happened. She said it was on the news and I didn't know anything about that. When Sam told me his father's death was on the news, I had to find out one more detail.

"Wait, was your father's killer Jamaican?"

"Yes," he replied.

I told him the story about camp that summer, and we both sat there in awe of how the counselor thought his father was mine. We were in two different places, but dealing with similar tragedies in different ways that same year.

When I was at the altar of the retreat years ago, and came and prayed for me, he had been mourning the loss of his own father a year and a half earlier. He told me his father's death hit him hard because he really didn't get the chance to bond with him as his other brothers had. He battled with his own salvation for many different reasons and found himself suicidal at one point. He was walking over a small bridge at night, and just like me, he thought of killing himself by jumping off.

My heart broke for Sam because he loved his dad, and he had died trying to be a hero. His dad's death rocked the church they attended because Manny was both an elder and pillar there. He was loved by everyone. His family was devastated by the loss of their hero and mentor. I knew this was confirming that God did not want my father to enter into eternity lost. Sam's father was the perfect candidate for a miracle, but God felt his time on earth was complete, where he gave my father 13 more months to change his life after his shooting.

Many people have been angry with God for allowing a child, or a loving mother to die while killers and murderers get to live. I have learned to trust God, even though I may not fully understand why He does what He does. I learned a long time ago that our ways are not His ways. His wish is to be reconciled with everyone because His desires are that none would perish. We, on the other hand, live with a mentality that the bad should die and the good should live. If we really think about it though, who among us is really good? We feel every liar, thief, murderer, home wrecker, abuser or molester should be killed because we have a warped way of categorizing sin. The truth, however, is that if we judge by those standards alone, none of us would be allowed to live. Deciding who should get mercy and who should be punished is a very hard line to draw. I believe if God allowed our form of justice to happen we would be even more disappointed with the results.

Sam missed his father for many years. He wished he had more time to spend with him to bond more with his dad, and to learn from him all he had to teach. To this day, Sam remembers the last goodbye he said to his dad, and he wishes that he did it with a hug.

Chapter 15

THE FIRST 8 STEPS

STEP ONE

A few days after our talk, Sam and I spoke about talking to my mother about getting married. We sat her down one night and told her we really loved each other and wanted to know what she thought about us getting married. There was more to the conversation, but overall she thought the whole thing was a joke. She did not take us seriously at all. She entertained the conversation for Sam's sake and didn't want to seem rude, but the look on her face told me everything.

After Sam left that night, my mother and I got into an argument because she felt I was too young. I was 18, and in her eyes, I only wanted to marry the very first guy I ever truly dated. My mother wasn't happy at all, and boy did she express it. She laughed at every excuse and idea I threw her way. I even told her God had spoken to me and told me we were meant to be together. I can see how saying that to her may have sounded stupid and juvenile. I even felt a bit awkward for saying that because I sounded like one of those girls who defended their young love to their parents just to find out it was nothing but a joke months later.

She went on to tell me Sam was not capable of taking care of me, and he wasn't driven enough to make a decent living. His idea of being an actor made her laugh even more than my idea of being a pastor. She said ministry didn't put food on the table, and when life hits me I would see things differently. She was the one taking care of me, so I didn't really understand the challenges of the world yet.

Then she finally said it.

"You know why you're doing this, because your father isn't here. If your father was here you would have never done this nonsense. You would have never thought to bring a kid like Sam into this house. If he was here, this talk of marriage would have never happened."

She was right, but not in the way she meant it. If my dad was there, I wouldn't have had any chance for a future. He would have stolen it, like he almost did. It was his death that gave me the chance to live. I wanted to look her in the eyes and say all the things he took from me, but instead I just left the room.

I stood my ground and was not going to let her take this moment away from me. I didn't care what she said. I was going to marry Sam one day. Her negativity did not cause me to doubt what I heard from God. There was still much for me to do and learn. Leaving to go back to school when the summer was over was a lot harder the second time around.

STEP TWO

Shortly after I went to back to Zion, Sam made the trip up to my school for my 19th birthday. With the help of some of my friends there, he proposed to me at a beautiful lakeside. In my mind, I thought this had to be some sort of game or dream. Was I really doing this? As soon as the ring was placed on my finger, doubt started filling in me. I didn't have time to indulge in these thoughts, I had to get my mind in the mode of school after he left.

The school had a policy that required every student to volunteer at a local church and get some hands-on experience in ministry. With the help of a friend from school, I was able to attend the church of Pastors Jim and Barbel Prior, a married couple who ran a small church in Rhode Island. Their church wasn't exactly around the corner, but my friend had a car and together we volunteered to serve alongside the Priors. They were both alumni of Zion Bible Institute, so they were very welcoming and loving to us.

I was only at their church for one year, but within that year Pastor Barbel and Pastor Jim taught me a whole lot. The members of their church weren't just congregational members, they were all one big family. Everyone loved each other and cared for one another. In Pastor Barbel, I found the sweetest, most patient, loving and kindest person there ever was. No better example of a virtuous woman existed than her. She had a smile that was infectious and a hug that could make anyone melt. She was so dedicated, and she had a passion for every soul that came into the doors of her church. Pastor Barbel was the mother of three small precious girls. I was drawn to her because her love was so real. It wasn't too long until I felt like part of their family. To this very day, she remains in my heart as the most loving and kindest person God has placed in my life.

Pastor Jim was the silent, but extremely observant type. When you thought he wasn't listening to you at all, he would chime into your conversation and prove to you he had been plugged in the whole time. He would remember things others would have easily forgotten and was an expert of the small details. He would use them to bring confirmation to whatever you were seeking answers for. Pastor Jim was precious to me because unlike the examples I had seen in the past, his wife was his partner. He did not rule her and she did not rule him, they were a team (Do you see what God was doing here?).

I was always shown in the past that the wife was silent, obedient and did as the husband said. She never participated in the services except to pray for the members at the altar or cook and clean up after an event. Pastor Jim showed me that did not have to be the case. The relationship they had, and still have, as husband and wife was a partnership and a team.

This concept worked well for them because as a team, when one was weak, the other was there to be strong.

They allowed me to work with their teens as I felt lead to. I became close to their three girls soon enough. The Pastors also had a close friend who lived next door. She was Pastor Barbel's best friend and the worship leader at the church, Gail. Talk about a woman full of joy. Gail had a heart that was, and is, so welcoming. She showed me so much love. She had two children, a boy and a girl, and I grew close to her daughter as well. At first, I questioned the idea of being able to work with teens, but my experience with these four precious girls gave me a little more encouragement to keep going in youth ministry. I grew to love them all and the church so much, and every opportunity I had to spend with them was a blessing to me. I grew to resent the distance between them and the school. I wanted to be there so much more than I was.

Sadly, my time with the Priors and their church, Lighthouse, was a very short one. I was not able to afford my full third year of school, so I decided to stay home and work. I made sure to stay close with the Prior's through phone calls and occasional visits. I eventually shared with Pastor Barbel my testimony of abuse. She was blown away at the things I had gone through, and with my permission, shared my story with others to whom she ministered. She asked me something I had never thought to do:

"Would you be willing to write down your testimony, because there are many who need to hear what you have to say?"

I had always seen my past as shameful, never as a way to minister to others. I thought about it, but I never really did anything about it. It would be quite awhile later that her words would echo back to me.

STEP THREE

Pastor J left my home church while I was in my first year of Zion. Before I left for Zion that first year, he informed me of his thoughts about leaving. He reminded me that when he first came, he said he was only going to be here for four or five years. He wanted to see the current generation of kids graduate before leaving. Sam and I did not go to the same church. My church was located in Queens, and his was located in the Bronx. His youth group was totally different from mine. They were more lively and a whole lot more talented than mine. There was also a lot of opportunity for ministry there. So after leaving school, I didn't feel as connected to my church as I did before. Many things had changed after Pastor J had left, and I started feeling God pull me to Sam's church.

Sam's youth group had a choir that would have blown your mind. They went all over the New York area ministering in churches, schools, and at outreaches. His youth pastor, Mitchell, was absolutely wonderful. He treated me like I was one of his teens, he and soon started mentoring me little by little, as he did for Sam. When Sam's dad had died, Pastor Mitch took Sam and his two older brothers under his wing as best he could. He taught Sam about drama and play writing among other things. As soon as I decided to stay home from school, I started traveling to the Bronx whenever I could to attend his church.

As Sam and I started dating, Mitch made it his business to know me on a more personal level. I grew to love him, and he soon became a great substitute for Pastor J who was no longer around. He gave me an opportunity for ministry as the Priors did. He strongly believed in taking your gifts and talents and using them for the Lord. He wanted every young person and young adult to operate at their fullest potential. I was given the privilege of singing with the choir. It was the best feeling to be a part of something again.

I began traveling with them, and that was a blessing. The impact we made as a group was something you could never get used to. It was amazing. I felt unworthy, but yet I also felt blessed to experience it all. Somehow Mitch found out about my testimony, and he asked me to take five minutes to share my testimony at an outreach one day. I seriously did not know what to do with myself. This was crazy, but awesome.

The time came for me to share in front of a crowd of strangers at a park. I felt so nervous I could have thrown up at that very minute, but God gave me the courage to share a small portion of my story. I can't remember everything I said, but I remember the faces of people as I told them about the pain I experienced living in my abusive home. I spoke about wanting to commit suicide and no longer wanting to live. I gave God all the honor and glory for bringing me this far, for giving me the hope of a future and a totally different life.

Even though I was very rough around the edges, Mitch encouraged me and gave me many opportunities to minister after that. He mentored me and helped me see my potential in so many areas. He even arranged for a van load of potential youth leaders to attend a Leaders Conference with him, and he asked me to join him on the trip. This trip was what sealed it for me. It made me feel I was officially at my new home church.

Pastor Mitchell believed God had called me to be a youth pastor, not the wife of a youth pastor. He invested in this belief more than I ever expected. He felt God was going to take me places, but I needed a lot of help and training. He saw something in me I truly did not see in myself. One thing about this man was that he was really good at finding out that special thing about you, and then doing everything he could to nurture it and promote growth. There was nothing he didn't think you could do if God was in the center of it all.

STEP FOUR

As Sam and I got closer to our wedding day, I became very scared of failure. All those thoughts from when I was in school started to come back. The idea of calling off the wedding was overwhelming me. Sam's family was very supportive of the wedding. His mother was such a loving person, and she did not think twice in making me feel I was the daughter she always wanted. She shared with me the love she had with Sam's father Manny. They had their rough moments, but by the end of their lives together they could not have been more in love, more dedicated or more passionate about one another.

Everything seemed perfect before Manny was taken from them. Her heart was still broken from the loss even as we spoke of him. Could I actually step into a family like this? I can't express how I felt drawn to disaster. I didn't feel I was worthy of having anything good. This was a good family with a serious reputation in their church. It was intimidating to say the least.

My family, on the other hand, felt I was rushing things with Sam. They thought that I needed to wait to finish school. One night, I decided to be honest with Sam and tell him I was very scared, almost too scared to continue on with the wedding. Our mothers had two different views of how our marriage would end up. My mother felt we were going to fail, but his mother felt in her spirit that I was the one to marry him.

I told him everything my mother had said, and that she was very clear about how she thought I didn't have what it takes to be a good wife. The idea that I would pursue youth ministry was a joke to her. She continued to feel that working in the church was not going to put food on the table. If there was anything negative my mother could say about our marriage, she said it. I explained to him how I stood my ground, but now I started believing her.

This was not a game to me. He was my first real boyfriend, so the question in my mind was would I have done this with the next guy as well? I started doubting every word I heard when I was in Zion. I told him if he wanted to back down and cancel the wedding I would understand. I was secretly hoping he would say yes. At least then we could go back to being two silly kids who enjoyed each other and nothing else.

But in Sam's love, he listened to it all. He also promised me that he was just as scared as I was. He admitted he didn't know if he could provide for me, or be able to be the man I needed him to be. What he did know, was that God had called both of us for something far greater than just two people coming together. To him, this was also about the many different lives God had entrusted to us as a couple. We both knew we were called into ministry, that was a no brainer. But he felt that apart from each other we would not have as big an impact as if we were married. Talk about a guilt trip.

We decided to do as Moses did and placed our feet into the water first, and then waited for them to part. On August 1, 1998, exactly six years after my father was buried, Sam and I got married. I was starting a new life with a new man. The journey we were about to begin was far greater than we could have ever thought. I heard someone say that an NFL star gets a ring when the games are over, but in marriage you get a ring when everything is about to begin.

STEP FIVE

God did not wait to use us as a couple. A month after our wedding, Pastor Mitch turned the drama ministry over to Sam. We were now responsible for one of the biggest productions the church did each year. The team consisted of about 30 full time members, and about 10 to 15 part time members. Sam and Pastor Mitch saw something I didn't see happening. In August of 1999, we were asked to be the new youth leaders of the church.

Eventually, Pastor Mitch established his own church not too far from us, and our church needed someone to take his place. No one could take this man's place! For over a decade of youth ministry, thousands of teens and adults had been ministered to by him. How could we fill those shoes? We were extremely intimidated, but Mitch was the one the current pastor went to for advice on who he would recommend to be the new leaders.

The board members of the church, and the current Senior Pastor, asked us to lead the youth as a <u>team</u>. Eventually, Sam was brought on to become the youth pastor at the church, and I stayed by his side the whole way. I was a pastor's wife now, the very thing I said I did not want to become. But I was not like the pastor's wives I saw growing up, I did exactly what I said I would do; I was his partner like Pastor Barbel was to

Pastor Jim. I refused to let him take on this huge task on his own. We did everything together, always.

STEP SIX

Sam and I had been married for six years when my relationship with my mother changed dramatically for the better. God healed my heart towards her in so many ways. She was not the same woman I grew up with. She had become my accountability partner in the faith, and she spent much of her time praying for Sam and I, our two children and our ministry.

My mother became the perfect intercessor for me. There were many challenges in the early stages of my marriage, along with the trials of ministry and motherhood. I needed her more than ever before, and she willingly stepped up to the plate. I was so glad to have her support during my journey of becoming a woman and a mother. I would never have been able to take on the role of Sam's wife and be a leader in the church if I did not have my mother praying intently for me. Where she was lacking in my childhood, she more than made up for in my adult years.

I recently had a meeting with one of my young adult girls from church. She expressed to me that once she leaves her home she will never need her parents again. I told her how wrong she was in thinking that. Parenting is not an 18 year job. It is a job that lasts a lifetime, and it evolves with every new stage of the child.

My mother taught me some things about mothering. Parenting was hard and I wanted to do it right. I didn't want to be like my father and abuse my children, even though that struggle was present. Just before I gave birth to my first child, I felt God calling me to be a stay-at-home mom. So I left my full time job in the city to give birth and never returned. That was a big struggle for me. After my second child was born I began to feel my life was very hectic and overwhelming. I was frustrated. I sought God for patience, but I felt He wasn't giving me any. I began to battle with depression again because life was turning out to be more challenging as the days went on. I truly wanted to get in the car and drive off with no thought of looking back, but the thought of driving away with my son not yet potty trained frightened me, so I put the idea on hold (I had issues).

It was in the midst of all this I received a call from my mom. We talked about what I was feeling, and then she told me something that changed me from the inside, in a good way.

"I'm so proud of you for staying at home with the kids," she said. "I wish I could go back in time and do it all over again. One moment I was changing diapers and preparing to put braids in your hair, and then all of a sudden, here you are, out of the house with your own kids. Where did the time go?"

It was here that I was able to tell her how I wished she had spent more time with us.

"If I knew that life was going to go so fast," she replied, "I would have spent more time with you and your brother.

Unfortunately, when you are in the moment, you can't see yourself doing anything else but changing diapers. You think it will never end, so you take it for granted."

I heard the softness in her voice.

"Don't rush them to grow up, don't fret, that child will learn to use the potty. Don't get worked up over things that will eventually happen. He will learn to eat his veggies, sleep in his bed and dress himself. Spend as much time as you can holding on to them while they can still be held. Don't fret about the dirt because dirt will always be there. But your babies are only babies for just a moment. Before you know it, they are leaving the house going off to college, getting married and having kids like you."

This conversation was one of many we had. They each brought with them a warm sense of healing to our relationship as we connected more.

STEP SEVEN

Even though I had quit my full time job, I was still working along Sam as much I could with the Youth Ministry. I led girls groups, and was the head of our Human Video/ Dance and Flags teams. God opened up doors we could never have opened on our own. He placed before us opportunities we never imagined. We watched as our church expanded and became one of the largest churches in the Bronx.

Our youth group consisted of over one hundred teens. In each service we averaged about eighty to eighty-five. Our ministry teams consisted of about forty teens, and they were all amazing. We were able to minister to people through drama and the arts. I could not believe how God was moving and how much He was allowing us to be used. Yes, The Lord did tell me about this in Zion, but this was a journey I did not see – or should I say, believe – could really happen. The young people we worked with became the fire that kept Sam and me going. We loved each of them, and they worked hard because they loved us in return.

During our time at this church, we were able to minister to hundreds of young people and adults. Our shows would be standing room only, and the church altars would be filled at the end of each presentation with people who wanted to give their hearts over to Christ.

All that truly blessed me, but the life changing moment for me was when I was asked to share my full testimony with the women of our church. I couldn't believe they wanted me to speak. I had never shared my testimony as a whole before, and I found it seriously intimidating.

I was honored to do so, but the first thing I needed to do was confront my mother. I couldn't take the chance of telling my testimony and her hearing about it from someone else. The last time we spoke about what my dad did to me it did not go over well. It was hard to find the right way to tell her about what I was asked to do because I didn't know what to expect from her. Was she going to be in denial, get mad or resentful?

"Mom, I wanted to talk with you because the Women's Ministry at church has asked me to give my testimony." There was silence, so I went on, "I wanted to talk to you about it first before I spoke."

"Well what are you going to tell them?" She asked.

I took a deep breath, "I am going to tell them about when I was molested. Did you know about Matthew molesting me?"

"Your father told me some things, but I wasn't clear about what actually happened. It was told to me as if it was just a rumor. No one told me what actually took place."

I decided to tell her everything that happened with him. I told her what he used to do and why I cried so badly when she would leave. I told her about him threatening to tell her I was bad so she wouldn't come and visit. She began to cry. My mother rarely cried and to hear her crying broke my heart and still does.

"This makes so much sense. I don't know if you remember, but we were constantly taking you to the doctor because you were getting infections. They thought it was the underwear, so we kept on buying different ones because we thought that was the problem. We didn't know all along it was because you were being molested. He was so cruel. How could he do that to you? This makes so much sense now."

As you already know, that part was not the only story in my testimony. I went on to tell her about the abuse dad use to inflict on me. I told her how he used to call me every name in the book, and of when he beat me in school. I told her about the time he stepped on my face and my chest.

I explained to her about the girls forcing me to do things to them in the bathroom, and how I had fights because of it. As I spoke, I provided her answers to certain things she did not understand all those years ago. She believed everything I said, and she even helped me put some pieces of my own puzzle back together. See, I had reached a certain point where I found it hard to remember, and my mind played off some things as if they had never happened. She helped confirm to me that all this really did happen, and I know it sounds like a bad thing, but all of it made me feel that I was not crazy. Finally, FINALLY!!!! I was able to let out and vent to her what I held in for so long.

After hearing everything I went through, and what I was going to share, my mom cried even more.

"Please forgive me. Please, I did not know these things were happening. Please don't hold these things against me. Forgive me, forgive me."

This was a breaking point for me. For so many years I thought my mother just didn't care. To hear her ask for forgiveness was so freeing for me. I never thought she would ask ME for forgiveness, but God knew what I needed, and exactly when I needed it.

God had done so much work in me, especially since now I was a mother as well. I knew I needed to give her the same grace and mercy that I may need if I ever make a life altering mistake with my own kids. My mother was my friend and my accountability partner. I was proud of how far she had come. By this time, she was not only going on ten years of returning to the Lord, but she was also a pastor of her own church. She was changing lives with her own testimony.

STEP EIGHT

It was time for me to move forward and use my testimony to help set people free. At the time I didn't see it exactly like that. I knew there were several women who had experienced abuse who would be attending, so I thought my story could help them find some hope.

It was July 2, 2005. It was a warm Saturday morning. My heart started beating so rapidly I thought my friends who came to support me could hear it. As I watched, woman after woman entered the sanctuary. I became increasingly over-whelmed by what I was about to do. Was I really ready to tell these people the heartbreaking story of being an abused young girl who defeated every demon and obstacle that held her back by the grace of God? Was I willing to be vulner-able? I had practiced saying parts of my testimony, and I had broken down each time. How was I going to keep my com-posure here? I knew for certain I was going to cry.

I thought I was going to throw-up when the head of the Women's Ministry got up to the pulpit and started the service. After making the necessary announcements, she looked at me and started giving me an introduction I was not expecting.

She told the ladies there about my service in the youth ministry, and about my times of ministering in drama and human video. When all was said and done, she called me up. I felt all the blood leave my face, my heart stopped beating and my mouth got really dry. I wanted to run to the bathroom, but it was way too late.

I stood at the podium looking across the sanctuary at all the faces of the ladies who came to hear this message. I saw women who I had not had the privileges of speaking with before on a one on one basis because of the size of our church. I saw teens from my youth group who came out to support their leader. I saw the familiar faces of my dear friends I had grown to know and love. Lastly, I looked in the balcony and saw the seats completely empty except three people – my two children and my dear husband who refused to miss this for the world.

I took a deep breath and started off with Isaiah 41:8-15 –

"But you, Israel, my servant,
Jacob, whom I have chosen,
you descendants of Abraham my friend,
I took you from the ends of the earth,
from its farthest corners I called you.
I said, 'You are my servant';
I have chosen you and have not rejected you.
So do not fear, for I am with you;
do not be dismayed, for I am your God.

I will strengthen you and help you;
I will uphold you with my righteous right hand. 'All who
rage against you
will surely be ashamed and disgraced;
those who oppose you
will be as nothing and perish.
Though you search for your enemies,
you will not find them.
Those who wage war against you
will be as nothing at all.
For I am the LORD your God
who takes hold of your right hand
and says to you, Do not fear;
I will help you.
Do not be afraid, you worm Jacob,
little Israel, do not fear,
for I myself will help you,' declares the LORD,
your Redeemer, the Holy One of Israel.
'See, I will make you into a THRESHING sledge,
new and sharp, with many teeth.
You will thresh the mountains and crush them,
and reduce the hills to chaff.'"
Isaiah 41:8-15 (NIV)

After reading this verse, I began telling my story. As
I spoke, I broke down and became a total mess. This was
the first time I had uttered these words to a large group of

people. I survived a very painful season in my life I thought was never going to end. I was showing them my scars and my wounds. I was allowing myself to be vulnerable to these women because I knew my pain would be their gain. I was willing to enter into that world all over again for the slightest chance of setting one person free from the same chains that once held me down.

When I took a moment to look at the faces in the crowd, I was met with watery eyes and runny noses. Many of these women were victims of the same kind of hurts I had once faced. They understood what it was like to be me, to be broken and ashamed. They knew what it was like to think their nightmares would never end. Some of them were still living in them. They knew about hopelessness and despair, because those were their companions regularly. They knew what it was like to want to die, but God continually was commanding life. They knew the feeling of pure rage and anger, because they had no control over their circumstances. I was speaking to the right group of women that day.

I went on to tell them of the important role my husband played in my life. I can tell you hands down the enemy did not think I was going to marry this loving, caring, patient man. Satan thought I was going to screw this up, but because I put God in the center, I was able to rise to the top. The fact that I trusted God to pick my mate was so important because I knew my flesh wanted someone else totally different. I know that for me, to find a man like Sam in the damaged state of mind I was in, and then be able to keep him was a miracle.

Many of the women sitting in that sanctuary had a different story. They found men who abused them because they only knew abuse. They didn't know how to live like a princess because they were always treated like trash. Some women passed up on the right man because they didn't feel worthy enough to have something good. My story was different, but I didn't end it there.

I shared my testimony for a reason, and I'm sharing it now with you in this book for the exact same reason.

Look at verse 15 of Isaiah 41:

"I will make you into a <u>threshing</u> sledge, <u>new and sharp</u>, with many teeth." (NIV)

A threshing sledge was a farm tool used for grain. God spoke of threshing a mountain and crushing them, making the hills into chaff. God did not call me to just have a husband and a few kids. He called me to be a weapon, His weapon. See, a threshing sledge was brand new, it was something that had never been seen before and it was powerful. God didn't want us to just move the mountains or climb over them, he wanted us to demolish them so they could never be in our way again.

God has called me to be a weapon that cannot be stopped. He has taken everything the enemy has thrown at me and built me up to be a "Threshing Sledge" for the Kingdom of God. Every insecure, impure, abusive, deadly, raging, painful, hurtful, embarrassing, shameful, disgusting moment of my life should have placed me in chains of bondage. But I write to you now as a free woman, a wife and a mother who serves the Lord Jesus Christ.

I never thought the day would arrive where I could say this, but those painful moments of my past are so precious to me now. They allowed me to find favor among those ladies. My hurts gave me the opportunity to be a powerful woman that day. The scripture God gave me long before in Genesis 50:20, *"You intended to harm me, but God intended it for good to accomplish what is now being done, the saving of many lives,"* made so much sense at that moment. The fact that God saw all this before He made me, caused me to love Him all the more. By the end of the message, I wasn't sure if there would be anyone who wanted to come up for prayer; but even if there was only one person who came up, that was fine.

I understand the power of investing in one life because if it wasn't for Brother and Sister Anderson inviting me to go with them to Sunday School so many years ago, I really believe I wouldn't be here. If my youth pastor had not adopted the role of a father for me seriously, I would not have been here. If it wasn't for Pastor Barbel and Pastor Jim mentoring me, trusting me and planting seeds in me, I would not have had the confidence I had in ministry. If it wasn't for Mitchell seeing my potential and watering the seeds the Prior's had planted in me, I would not have held on to the dream of Youth Ministry. If it wasn't for Sam being my companion and my biggest cheerleader, I could not have had the courage to go the distance with God.

I was blessed to see several women come up to the altar. They wanted to be this same weapon I talked about. They were tired of being victims. They wanted to be victors. I cried with several of them that day. They thanked me and embraced me with such love and appreciation for my willingness to share this side of myself. It was then I was able to say wholeheartedly to God,

"If you allowed me to go through this for the salvation of others, then so be it. I would do it all over again for the saving of souls."

Chapter 16

SOME LAST THOUGHTS

*I*t has been my pleasure to minister to thousands of young people and adults. My husband and I have been able to mentor and pray for many people in our sixteen years of ministry. God has opened doors for us to be in full time ministry, in order to help others facing difficult challenges in life. We have been so blessed to see many lives transformed by the grace of God.

In writing this book, I hope to reach more people by way of testimony, and to share about the Lord as an extension of my service to God's people. As I stated before, I do not write for sympathy or for any other reason, except that you the reader may be blessed in knowing there is a God who loves you. He is working all things for those who are truly seeking His face and He has a purpose for each and every one of us. I took a major step of faith with sharing even more details of my past with you than I had planned because I know my testimony, as yours, is a weapon that can be used against the enemy.

All the "hell on earth" I experienced in my life, I know was used to draw me further away from the Lord. If the enemy knew I was going to use those times of trials and struggles as a way to draw closer to God, he would have left me alone years ago. He never thought I would rise up from the ashes of these battles, so he kept coming at me, hitting me with blow after blow. He placed mountains in front of me he thought were too big for me to move or even climb over. But to his surprise, with God's help, I made it through. The bigger the mountain, the sharper God made me. And every time I wake up and put my feet to the floor in the morning, I cause a quake in hell.

I don't know what your purpose is in reading this book, but I need you to know I am praying for you. I have also asked others whom I trust to pray for you as well. We are praying for God to reveal His plans for you, and I want the Lord to do even greater things in you than what He has done in me. My soul has been so heavy during the process of putting this book together, and it's because I know people out there are hurting and are looking for answers. For that reason, I allowed myself to remember and relive those things I would have loved to have forgotten.

Before we end our time together, I want to leave you with some Scriptures that have been a real blessing to me, and I pray they will be a blessing to you as well.

<u>God Saw It All From The Beginning</u>

"'Before I formed you in the womb I knew you, before you were born I set you apart; I appointed you as a prophet to the nations.' 'Alas, Sovereign L<small>ORD</small>,' I said, 'I do not know how to speak; I am too young.' But the L<small>ORD</small> said to me, 'Do not say, 'I am too young.' You must go to everyone I send you to and say whatever I command you.'" Jeremiah 1:5-7 (NIV)

From the very beginning, before you were a thought in your parents' minds, before the pregnancy test said positive, God knew who you were. He knew everything you would go through, and He knew every struggle you would have. God was not disappointed by your failure, and He was not surprised by your victories either. He knew you and called you for great things. Don't think that any opportunity is too small. Speaking to one person is just as important as ministering to 2000 in a stadium. Remember, I am here because of two people who invited me to church, who to this day, do not know what happened to me. There is no task God will place before you without equipping you for it. You have been called to be a prophet to the nations, sharing and proclaiming His Word to all who will listen. Don't bother telling Him about your shortcomings, as if they are reasons why you cannot be used. The Lord uses our weaknesses as proof of His power, and allows us to overcome our obstacles despite the odds that lie against us, in order to reach nations.

<u>Be Strong and Courageous</u>

"Be strong and courageous, because you will lead these people to inherit the land I swore to their ancestors to give them. Be strong and very courageous. Be careful to obey all the law my servant Moses gave you; do not turn from it to the right or to the left, that you may be successful wherever you go. Keep this Book of the Law always on your lips; meditate on it day and night, so that you may be careful to do everything written in it. Then you will be prosperous and successful." Joshua 1:6-8 (NIV)

Whether you know it or not, God has called you to lead. It doesn't matter if you are a pastor or if you are a single parent, you have people before you who need to be lead to the knowledge of Christ and His salvation. We are God's ambassadors, and as such, we are called to reach out to the lost and dying. It is not a role that should be taken lightly. When Joshua chose to learn under Moses, he didn't do it with the idea that he would become the next leader. He did what he knew was right, and God honored him for it.

We have no idea what God has planned, which is why we must make sure to be where He has called us to be. It can be a bit scary when you think God has ordained you to lead people into the promise land, but like he told Joshua, we are to remain strong and courageous, keeping the word of the Lord in our mouths. The Bible is our blueprint for success in the Kingdom, and it holds within its pages the answers to all our questions that need answering. We just need to know how to look.

You Will Understand Later

"Jesus replied, 'You do not realize now what I am doing, but later you will understand.'" John 13:7 (NIV)

Doesn't this verse sum up our lives as a whole with Jesus? This should be the poster verse for every Christian. There will be times, if you have not yet had them, when we will have absolutely no idea what Jesus is doing and why. This verse takes place when Jesus was about to wash the feet of the disciples. Peter asked Him, "Jesus what are you doing?" Jesus gave His response, and in verse 8 Peter then tells Him, "No, You shall never wash my feet." Christ was trying to teach his disciples an important lesson that would benefit them on their mission in the future. In their eyes, however, Jesus was positioning Himself as the lowly, disrespected, disgraceful foot-washing servant. There was no honor in that. They did not understand the circumstances. In fact, as we read the story, we see they had no clue about what was to come in a matter of hours. They did not know their lives would be completely different by this time tomorrow.

"But later you will understand," He told them. They were going to need each other. They were going to have to learn to be humble for the task that lay ahead of them. They needed to learn how to trust in the One who taught them, and believe He was not going to leave them on their own. In our own situations, we may not realize God is remaking us and cleaning us up. At times, we think He has forgotten us or is ignoring us. Sometimes we are convinced He doesn't even know what He is doing.

I hold a high respect for this verse. It was actually the verse God gave me before this book was even a thought in my mind. Very briefly, allow me to share one last piece of my testimony with you. In my time of prayer and devotion with God, He asked me to remove some people from my life who were going to be a distraction to me and a stumbling block to what He had planned next for me. This made no sense to me, because the ones He told me to pull away from had been my closest friends for nearly fifteen years. Some of them understood, while other did not. They felt I had other motives. It was hurtful to them and it was heart-wrenching for me. I did not know why I needed to do this and why I needed to do it in this way.

All that God kept saying to me was that there are people I would minister to, but I needed to be obedient FIRST, He would bring understanding later. It was so painful. At the time I thought it was so unnecessary, but NOW I understand. In the months that followed, I saw what God was doing and why, but I only saw this because I obeyed Him. Without exposing too much, had I not listened, this book would not have been written or published.

If you don't have John 13:7 highlighted in your Bible, stop reading, get a highlighter and highlight it! Put stars around it, get little tiny light bulbs and glue them there so when you open your Bible they blink at you . . . okay maybe not the lights, but at least highlight it. It will serve as a great reminder for when your days of "not understanding" come – and they will.

Keep Trusting Him

"However, as it is written: 'What no eye has seen, what no ear has heard, and what no human mind has conceived the things God has prepared for those who love Him.'" 1 Corinthians 2:9 (NIV)

I cannot explain how many times I needed to be reminded that God's way was the best way. To "Love" God is to obey God. To "Love" God is to follow God. To "Love" God is to honor God. To "Love" God is to trust God. You have to trust that He holds you in His hands, and that He will not allow this world to overpower you. You need to believe nothing around you can compare to what God has for you. Your hard situations and struggles are not going to last forever.

<u>Understand Your Calling</u>

"The Spirit of the Sovereign LORD is on me,
because the LORD has anointed me
to proclaim good news to the poor.
He has sent me to bind up the brokenhearted,
to proclaim freedom for the captives
and release from darkness for the prisoners,
to proclaim the year of the LORD's favor
and the day of vengeance of our God,
to comfort all who mourn,
and provide for those who grieve in Zion
to bestow on them a crown of beauty
instead of ashes,
the oil of joy instead of mourning,
and a garment of praise
instead of a spirit of despair.
They will be called oaks of righteousness,
a planting of the LORD
for the display of his splendor." Isaiah 61:1-3 (NIV)

Lastly, realize you have a calling. We are called to spread the Good News of Jesus Christ. There are those around you who are emotionally and spiritually poor. They need to know there is hope in this world, and you are the one God has anointed for the task of telling them. Your story may help to mend the hearts of many broken people. Your testimony may help to set people free. People are empowered when they hear others' stories, especially when they are stories they can relate to. There were many wonderful testimonies I heard throughout the years, but the ones that impacted me the most were those of people to whom I was able to relate.

THANK YOU FOR LISTENING

I pray this book was able to help encourage you, and that it was used to help you find freedom from any bondages of your past. In sharing a small portion of my story, I hope you were able to see the MIGHTY GOD I serve. As I stated before, this was not easy for me to write. The process stirred up things in me I found really hard to confront. But, this book was not about me, it was about God and about faith. I wrote it out of pure obedience, and I now place it in His hands.

I ask you to allow God to use you. Don't walk in your faith afraid of every corner you come up to. Find comfort in His arms and in His Word. Be a person with a heart for the lost and wounded. Believe that He has called you to greater things, and never let yourself become a victim of the enemy.

If you aren't already, begin attending a church that teaches and ministers the Word. Don't be fooled or taken in by how well the singers sing, or by how flashy the lights are. Pay attention to the heart of the leadership there. Do they challenge their people to read the Bible? Do they help them interpret the Word? When you find that, get involved. Become a student and learn. Be a new shaped Threshing Sledge for the Lord, and beat down those mountains.

AFTERWORD

*O*ne of the biggest regrets my mother had was not giving her life over to the Lord sooner. She ended up telling me why she didn't give her life over to God until after my father had passed on. Back in Jamaica, my mother had dedicated her life to The Lord. She regularly went to church and her life was centered on God. As she got older, she started partying. She began living a life different than how she was raised, and she eventually backslid. After meeting my father, she continued doing her own thing, but she felt the pulling of the Holy Spirit the whole time.

After I was born, they lived in a rental house that was converted into a church every Sunday. Whether my parents wanted to or not, we all went to church on Sundays as a family. One morning, the message was so compelling that my mother went to the altar to rededicate her life. After church was over, my father threatened her. He said that if she ever became a Christian he would leave her, and he would take me and my brother James away from her. With fear of losing her

291

family, she told God she wanted nothing to do with Him any longer. She was so in love with my father, and she was willing to walk away from God rather than lose him or her kids.

The act of choosing her family over God made her think she had blasphemed the Holy Spirit. Time went by, and she wanted to pray and ask for God's forgiveness. But she remembered several messages preached to her as a child:

"But whoever blasphemes against the Holy Spirit will never be forgiven; they are guilty of an eternal sin." Mark 3:29 (NIV)

People had taught this verse as a way to scare others so much they would not turn away from God. For my mother, that method of teaching kept her from thinking she could ever go back to Him. It convinced her she had blasphemed against the Holy Spirit, and her heart was grieved because there was no turning back now. She felt she had been doomed to eternal damnation because of her choice. She wrestled daily with the thought of God not forgiving her, and that she was ultimately going to go to hell. I was not aware of any of this at all.

I told her when I was younger and going to church that I regularly prayed for her. My mother told me she felt those prayers when I was a kid. She felt she couldn't give in, even though she wanted to, because of how she had FALSELY been taught that Scripture. It was harder for her when James came to live with us because he and I would witness to her, and she would desire salvation, but the enemy was always right there reminding her she had blasphemed against God.

During the last 13 months of my father's life, my parents were going to another church every Sunday. My mom said my father wanted to change so badly. He stopped smoking and cut back on his drinking. He was reading his Bible, and all they played at home was Christian music. As she told me this, that memory came back to me. I didn't remember my father had gotten rid of all the old reggae music and replaced it with Christian music. He did everything he could to cut loose all those friends who weren't good influences.

My mom explained to me that they used to go to parties a lot, I didn't know about that, but apparently they did. The Christmas before my father passed away, my mother promised God that was going to be her last party. She was going to live her life differently after that day. All of this was going on while I was praying for my mother's salvation.

When my father passed away, she was so lost in her thoughts. She knew she couldn't go on without God. One Sunday, she was so hurt and full of grief that she went to the altar to rededicate her life. She didn't remember the whole thing about blaspheming the Holy Spirit, she was too desperate at that moment. After she went home that day, my mother said the thoughts started flooding her mind again.

"What did you do? You can't get saved, you blasphemed remember? You're going to hell."

These thoughts replayed over and over in her mind. That day she went to the park with one of my aunts and Peter. She decided to bring her Bible with her for some reason. She needed answers from the Word. She had no particular Scripture in mind to begin with, but when she opened the Bible, the very first verse her eyes fell on was *Matthew 7:11* –

"If you, then, though you are evil, know how to give good gifts to your children, how much more will your Father in heaven give good gifts to those who ask him!" (NIV)

God needed her to know if she would never treat her own children with malice and contempt, then why would He? If she would forgive her children, why wouldn't God? He loved her, and He used this verse to help her see that. My mother who was in bondage for almost 20 years, was set free with that one verse. After that day, my mother never doubted her walk with God again.

ACKNOWLEDGEMENTS

I wanted to take some time to thank some people that have played such a major part in where I am today. First thank you to my husband and children for all their love and support through it all. Sam, you have been the perfect example of God's love to me. You never judged me or tore me down while I was healing from these wounds. You held my hand, prayed with me and even cried with me. God was right when he said he had something better for me. To my children, my Warrior, my Love, the Truth and the Presence of God...when you read this, I pray you will understand the God you serve. I pray that you will know that I love you tremendously. Thank you for being understanding while mommy was busy typing and crying.

To my family, Mom you will continue to be my inspiration and my joy. You are my accountability partner and my intercessor. I would not have this any other way. I love you and it's not how you start a race that matters, it's how you finish it. You are amazing and you have surely made up for all the mistakes made in the past. To my brothers, we have been through much and we have come out on the other side. I love both of you so much and I know more than anything, that you love me. Your love is so real and I am fortunate to have two brothers that would do absolutely anything for me.

To our youth pastors, Pastor J...there aren't words that can express how your love saved me. I cannot explain how I have tried to love my own youth as you loved me. You did the best you could with what you knew and I need you to know that I will never ever forget you. Mitchell Torres, I need to thank you for being such a great youth pastor to Sam and I. You were a great father figure to Sam when he didn't have one and he has followed in your footsteps with his own congregation. I have to say that you were the perfect person to come into my life and extract those things I did not know I had within me. You saw something I did not see and no matter how I fought you, plant seeds in me that have matured today. I owe you more than you know. We both love you guys and your lives shows the importance of investing in young people even if it's ONE.

To Pastor Jim and Barbel Prior, we owe you so much. For the last 18 years you have prayed for us, mentored us and encouraged us. You saved my life (literally) by your prophetic words and for that I must make my life count. We will always be Lighthouse's Missionaries to the world. Your prayers have propelled us into this life of ministry and we cannot over look that. Please don't stop praying because it has just started.

To Elizabeth Madaia and Lauren Anderson, man do I love you. You have laughed with me, cried with me and DANCED with me. We have chased lions together and made circles together. Thank you for allowing God to use you to prepare me for this. Also thank you to my Ladies that stuck by me when they had no idea what was going on. I know it was a hard season but you refused to give up and allow the enemy to have his way. You're my family always and I am rich because of you all.

To Monkey and Titi… "Well behaved women rarely make history". Your words and support mean more than you know.